The Champion: How to be Mentally and Physically Fit to Win

Peter D. Campbell

Herodotus Press

First published 2016

This edition was first published in 2016

Copyright © Peter Campbell 2016

The moral right of the author has been asserted

Published by Herodotus Press,
www.HerodotusPress.com

ISBN 978-0-473-35506-7

Published in New Zealand

About the author

Peter D. Campbell is a journalist and sports consultant. He was born in Australia in 1983 and grew up in New Zealand where he developed a love for sport and the great outdoors enjoying sailing and tramping.

Peter has competed competitively in sport throughout his childhood and adult life. He fences at a national level in New Zealand with a ranking often within the top 15 in the country.

Peter's interests include psychology, languages and sport. He enjoys travelling and does his best to live parallel lives in New Zealand and Europe. The author is a keen fencer and sailor.

In addition to his writing, Peter runs an NLP consultancy service Mind Design Ltd.

For more information visit his website at www.PeterDCampbell.com.

Other works by Peter D Campbell

Language Learning Secrets Revealed
In My Brother's Shadow
Purrfect Tales
The Prostitute and the Beggar
The Prodigal Son
The Blizzard by Alexander Pushkin (translation)
The Shot by Alexander Pushkin (translation)

Keep up to date with Peter D Campbell's writing at www.PeterDCampbell.com and on Facebook at www.facebook.com/PeterDCampbell.

Table of Contents

Introduction: My experience hacking my brain for sporting success 13

The Nature of the Subconscious 22

Basic principles of sporting success 29

Goal setting and motivation 33

Strength and fitness training 44

    Consistency trumps speed 47

    Developing super muscle 48

    Exercises 48

    Dips 53

    Holds 54

    Lifting exercises 55

    Running 56

    The Beep test 58

    The Cooper Test and Vo$_2$ Max 59

    Vo$_2$ Max fitness tables 60

    Skipping 61

    The "train-to–fatigue" controversy 61

    Advantages of training to fatigue 62

    Rest and constant training 64

Diet and nutrition 67

    Calories per day.. 69

How to train for your sport 71

    Learning new skills 71

    When learning a new skill 72

    General training... 75

    Prototype training session................................ 77

Visualisation and mental rehearsal 78

    How it works... 79

    Ways to visualise 81

    Basic visualisation... 82

Anchoring: Getting into the flow and emotional control 86

    Installing anchors 89

    To create an anchor 92

    Using anchors 92

    How anchors can help you 94

Develop resilience **96**

    Becoming a Navy SEAL 98

    Potterat's formula for resilience 99

    Increase resilience with anchoring 100

Dealing with trauma **102**

    Overcoming traumatic experiences 105

    When to use the trauma cure 107

    Recovering from injuries 108

    Other visualisations for injury recovery 111

Unlearning bad habits and installing good ones **114**

    To unlearn a habit 115

    To install a habit 115

    How I learnt to serve 116

Increasing speed **119**

    Muscle type 120

    Practice 122

Perception of time 122
Time distortion 124
   Techniques for learning from others and increasing speed 127

Beliefs 130
Changing beliefs 135

Performance personality and masks 141
Masks 142

Self-sabotage 145
Parts integration 148

Self talk 153
Changing the voice in your head 155

Hypnosis and sport 157
Everyone goes into trance 160
Self-hypnosis inductions 162
Hypnotic induction 163
Suggestions 166
Concluding a hypnotic suggestion 173
Using anchoring to improve hypnosis 175

Pain relief **177**
    Other techniques for pain control 180
    Parts Integration for pain control 181
    Changing the pain 184
    Altering representation of pain 185
    Final notes on pain control 187

Altering perceptions of reality **189**

Training diaries **193**

Competition **196**
    Nutrition 200
    Competition day 201
    Winning 203

Conclusion: putting it all together **207**

Appendix 1: Exercise Tables **209**
    Basic exercise plan 209
    Military fitness standards 210
    US Navy SEALS entry requirements 212
    US Ranger recommended scores 212
    SAS in camp regime 213

Basic Running plan 215
Intermediate Running plan............................ 216
   Twelve Week Running Plan for Marathon Performance - Advanced Runners............ 217
Beep Test Levels 218
Organisations' beep test levels 219

Appendix 2: Diet and nutrition........................ 221
Daily protein requirements 221
Carbohydrates 225
Snacks for recovery after training 226
Calories 228
Recommended dietary intake 229

Appendix 3: Visualisation Techniques 231
Installing anchors 231
Potterat's recipe for resilience: 235
Trauma recovery: 235
To unlearn a habit 238
Time distortion: 239
Belief changes 240
Masking 241

Parts integration 243
Changing the voice in your head 247
Hypnotic induction 248
Hypnotic Suggestions 250
Parts Integration for pain control 257
Altering representation of pain 261
Alter subconscious perception: 263

Bibliography and further reading..................... 266

Introduction: My experience hacking my brain for sporting success

Sporting talent is nothing more than having the right psychological make up, the right training and the right coach – and all of these elements can be learnt and acquired. This book will show you exactly how to do this.

This book is largely the result of learning a sport incorrectly. I was a natural at sport, most types of sport came easily to me. Being naturally lean, fast, strong and highly motivated, I expected to succeed at a national and possibly even international level. Having played tennis and hockey in childhood, I took up fencing at university, and although my talent was recognized, and although I trained hard, it never took me anywhere. I became a competent fencer but nothing remarkable – even on a provincial level. After graduating from university I went overseas, seeking a life of danger and adventure

The Champion

and finding both, returned home, older, wiser and with a few scars to remind me of youthful bravado.

I attempted to take up fencing again, but despite still being fit and strong I was dogged with injuries, injuries which I later learnt could easily have been avoided by doing a month of physical training to correct muscle imbalances.

At some stage I studied neuro-linguistic programming and learnt the basic principles which are applied to sports psychology and then drifted back into amateur sport, starting first with hockey and social tennis and then drifting into competitive fencing.

This time my fencing career was more successful. My coach was more focused and I spent time developing not only the physical and tactical side of the sport but also on developing psychological techniques to improve my sporting performance. This was a process of trial and error with the occasional disastrous mistakes leading to some awful results – but there were also successes. During this time I also ran a small consultancy in which I provided sports psychology services to a range of sportspeople, one of whom had recently been grounded by his key sponsor after he had lost his nerve and his form. I worked with him for a couple of hours and in the next major national competition he came third in the country when previously he had been failing to finish in the top ten.

Meanwhile my own sporting performances were improving. My fencing ranking moved into the top division and some of the country's best fencers were starting to take me seriously.

It was at this point that I was inundated with so much work that I was unable to train. And I stopped training almost entirely – I touched a weapon only about five times in six months. Despite this lack of physical training I continued to focus on the mental side of the sport using NLP techniques and visualizations I had developed from therapy for sporting applications.

Despite this haphazard approach to training I travelled to the tournament with no expectations – I was unfit, I had put on close to ten kilograms in the previous six months, and having had little practice I expected my opponents to run rings around me.

I reached the tournament and looked at the draws for the pools. I was ranked somewhere in the middle with someone of about my skill level, a few people whom I could expect to beat, the national champion and the previous tournament champion. I expected the latter two to clean me

The Champion

up, but I had a fair chance with the rest even out of training.

I warmed up, did my standard preparation which included visualization and anchoring techniques discussed in this book and then in an act of desperation I did something a little bit different.

As part of my NLP training, I had learnt hypnosis, a skill which comes in handy surprisingly often and while travelling to the tournament had been amusing myself by reading a book on stage hypnosis. In particular, I had just read a section on about a standard stage hypnotist trick where a hypnotized subject is instructed to stiffen like a plank of wood, and with his shoulders and ankles supported on two chairs is placed in a horizontal position and can then take the full body weight of a grown man, a task which usually only gymnasts perform.

I knew I was unfit and weak, and in my desperation I reasoned that if such feats of strength were possible when hypnotized on the stage, why shouldn't they be possible to me when I was competing? I found a quiet corner and hypnotized myself, giving myself instructions to be strong and to fence well. I didn't expect this to work – a fencing bout is more complicated than simply becoming a stiff plank; besides, I knew my main opponents and they were quite out of my league.

A fencing competition will usually start with pools where we fight to the first of five points and then once we have fought it out with five or six opponents, we then go into direct elimination which consist of bouts to 15. My first few pool bouts were against weaker opponents and provided little challenge to me. Then I came up against the reigning tournament champion and got three lucky hits in row. We were both surprised by this. Then he scored a point. Then I scored another two lucky points. I had won 5:1. A convincing win by anyone's standards. I was exhilarated. Adrenalin rushed through my system and I was so worked up that I could barely control myself in my next bout against someone who was approximately my equal. My hand was shaky and I found it hard to concentrate on my current bout. I decided that this was no time for finesse and as an epeeist finesse isn't always necessary. I fought the bout but in comparison to the previous one, I felt as if I were bludgeoning my opponent to death. I beat him 5:3, the most points I had given away so far in the competition.

My next bout was against the national champion. By this stage I had taken control of my emotions and was properly focused on my fencing and on

The Champion

him. We never completed the bout – we fought for the full time limit and he was up 4:2. I was stunned. I knew that half a year before, he would have defeated me in short order. Either everyone was having a bad day, or my new regime of non-training was working wonders!

The pools over I wandered to the information board where seedings and the draw were posted and took a double take. I was sitting happily in fifth place just behind the best fencers in the country.

That was the high point of the tournament. In the direct elimination I was put against a lowly seed that I would clean up easily. Hypnosis may have done wonders for me but it couldn't hold back the lack of preparation. I was still unfit, I hadn't been eating for high performance and my success was so unexpected I was finding it difficult to stay focused. I lacked energy throughout the bout and lost. It was a sorry end to a remarkable beginning but I was so astonished by my success earlier that day that I still felt like a victor. Next time, things would be different.

Shortly after this competition I left the country and again found myself in a position where I could not train. Instead I did the next best thing, I spent time reading and contemplating my approach to training and sport. I talked with other athletes and collated this information.

I had three main questions I wanted to answer:

- How do I train regularly to have the strength and fitness to achieve high performance goals?
- How do I eat to support this training?
- What are the best ways of learning skills quickly?
- How do I apply sports psychology to get the best out of my performance?

While the books I read on strength training and nutrition were full of useful information, I noticed that the books on sports psychology and performance were lacking. They did have useful information in them but much of it covered only the most elementary basics of what can be achieved using visualization techniques – while other techniques such as anchoring and hypnosis are completely ignored with a focus on mindfulness training and meditation. Furthermore, books tend to focus on only one element of sport. A book will be about physical training or nutrition or resilience or performance or visualization or hypnosis. There are no books that succinctly

The Champion

combine all these elements, which are critical for succeeding at sport.

Furthermore, many athletes are held back by their coaches not providing them with sufficient information, or by not having a set development plan. This book is intended to provide you with all the information you need to succeed in your sport. While the emphasis is on mental techniques and visualization techniques to improve performance, it also covers the basic information you need:

- to make yourself strong, fit and healthy (without paying expensive gym fees or personal trainers),
- for workouts and nutrition.

It teaches you how to:

- set your sporting goals,
- plan strategically to achieve your goals
- apply psychological principles for learning new skills and techniques

The Champion is designed as a guide so that you can teach yourself to be a high performing athlete, it can be used for additional information if you are working with a coach, or for you to train independently of a coach.

Peter D. Campbell

The Champion is useful for athletes of any level.

The Champion

The Nature of the Subconscious

The human brain has traditionally been split into two parts – the conscious mind and the subconscious mind. The conscious mind is largely responsible for analysis, logical thought, risk assessment, and short term memory. The subconscious does everything else. It is the subconscious that shoots you full of adrenalin when the neighbour's dog suddenly barks at you from behind the fence as you walk past. It is the subconscious mind that controls your pulse so that you get enough oxygen to your muscles and your brain. The subconscious controls all of the functions of your body that you are usually unaware of. When performing sport at a high level most of our actions are subconscious, and when we are in the "zone" we are often aware of nothing except the movement of our bodies – and this awareness often comes afterwards. In order to succeed at sport, we must not only train our bodies but also our minds. By learning to communicate directly with our subconscious we can speed up skill acquisition and can overcome performance related issues such as anxiety, nervousness and fear.

The body executes what the brain thinks. The ideas, images and words that we use affect the way we perform. Therefore the mental approach we use and the way we think about sport, life and our place in the world in general affects our success. If we lack self-confidence, feel downtrodden and a failure, we are much less likely to aim high and put in the effort necessary to succeed. Such people are less likely to be a success in life whether in sporting performance or professional careers.

This is far from being a one-way process. The way we perform affects the way we think, act and behave. People who have always considered themselves failures can suddenly turn over a new leaf by unexpected success. There are both mental-physiological links and physiological-mental connections.

A good example of these links between the mental and the physical demonstrate this point. Some years ago I was running in a half-marathon with an injured knee, while my other knee was in a pretty bad state as a result of favouring the injured one. I doubted that I would be able to

The Champion

complete the 22 kilometres. Having read a little at this stage about sports psychology I began the race repeating a mantra to myself "slow and easy". As I ran competitors overtook me one after another until my competitive instinct became aroused: I might be injured but that didn't mean I liked losing any more than I usually did! So I made one simple alteration to my mantra. I changed it to "fast and easy". Injured, I made no conscious effort to increase my speed. I simply repeated over and over again "fast and easy". The road took us up hill and as we ran I began overtaking people, one by one – repeating all the time "fast and easy". By the time I reached the downhill section I had lost track of my rivals. There was no one within sight behind me, nor could I see the leaders ahead of me. When I reached the finish I came in sixth out of 92 competitors. I have little doubt that in some strange way changing the mantra from "slow and easy" to "fast and easy" was a significant element in me doing so well despite my injured knees.

Our body carries out the instructions given by our brains. These range from simple actions such as opening and closing your hand to complex movements. Mostly we are unaware of these processes. They occur at a subconscious level and we are fortunate that on a basic level much of our activities are performed this way. If we had to consciously think about breathing while trying to maintain a conversation most of us would keel over dead within a few minutes. However, when performing in any competitive arena we often need to train our bodies and our minds to carry out complex tasks effectively and well, and better than our opponents. This book will teach you techniques for training your mind and body effectively so that you improve your performance, and we will do so by teaching you key skills for communicating with your subconscious mind.

Ideas and thoughts are constantly communicated to the subconscious. To some extent these ideas are filtered through the conscious mind (or more precisely through the pre-frontal lobe, which checks whether ideas fit our current beliefs and knowledge about ourselves and the world), those ideas which our conscious mind considers plausible are then passed through to the subconscious. These ideas are transmitted through such media as images, sounds, words and feelings. Often there will be a combination of feelings, sounds and images associated with every idea thus creating a sense of context and meaning for an individual situation. Ideas which are often repeated tend to be slowly absorbed by the subconscious and this is why practice is important, and is also how advertising often works. We can therefore deliberately use images, sounds, feelings and words to programme ourselves to achieve results that we desire. A knowledge of these principles will also help you avoid learning bad habits and adopting negative ideas about yourself.

Self-talk is one example of how we talk to ourselves and while our subconscious might ignore some of what we say, often we repeat the same phrases over and over again, establishing a new belief which in the case of middle level athletes is often negative. A good example of negative self-talk is the tennis player who misses a shot:

"How did I miss that one? I always miss the easy ones."

A few minutes later he misses another shot and answers his initial question: "It's the pressure. I always crack when the pressure is on."

At this point the game starts to fall to pieces and unless the player manages to get his act together, he loses. Furthermore, a player who has such an experience early in his career is likely to bring this experience to other tournaments and competitions with ideas (or beliefs) that he "always misses the easy ones" and that he "always cracks when the pressure is on". These statements became self-fulfilling prophecies and unless the player does something to contradict them they will continue to affect performance. This book will teach you not only to avoid establishing bad beliefs, but to change old ones.

Pointing exercise

While anecdotes and research are a good way of demonstrating the effectiveness of these techniques, trying them for yourself is the best way of convincing yourself that they work. So, in a spirit of curiosity, try the following:

1. Stand up and find a space where you can move comfortably without banging into anything; a metre around you should be sufficient.
2. Extend your right hand and point in front of you.
3. Without moving your arm, twist your body as far as it goes.
4. Note where your arm is now pointing, and return to your initial position.
5. Now imagine yourself doing the exercise again, imagine doing it easily and

The Champion

comfortably and twisting much more easily and much further.

6. Now point your arm in front again, and twist again.
7. Note how much further you twisted this time.

Peter D. Campbell

Basic principles of sporting success

Talent goes a long way in sport, but without the appropriate training, preparation and support it is often wasted. Success in sport more often than not comes down to determination and having had the good luck to come across a coach who is competent and who works to your strengths and overcomes your weaknesses so they don't handicap you. If you want to succeed in sport it is helpful to have the following:

- Have the right goals: goals are important to motivate you, they should be challenging but attainable and they should excite you. Furthermore, goals give you direction to focus your energy and determine your tasks. If you have the wrong goals you may fail to achieve them, or you might achieve them and discover that you actually wanted something else.

The Champion

- Have the right physical preparation: physical strength and fitness are important to any athlete regardless of the sport, whether it is chess, golf, archery, taekwondo or football. Being strong enough and fit enough to compete at a high level can often make up for other failings, while a lack of fitness or strength can let you down even if you are technically perfect in your sport. Knowing how to exercise to achieve your sporting goals is an essential part of your preparation.

- Have the right technical preparation: if you have poor technique your opponents will take advantage of it. Learn correct technique from the start (this might require physical preparation before you even start learning the sport to ensure you have the strength or fitness to execute the techniques correctly).

- Have the right psychological make-up. This includes determination, resilience, motivation, calmness, confidence, and your beliefs about yourself and your sport. A good coach will often instil the right mind set for the sport. This is one reason why training children and teenagers to be successful at sport is easier than adults:

they are more impressionable and therefore their personalities are more easily moulded into a winning mind set. **This book is designed to enable you to develop the winning mind set, regardless of age.**

- Optimism and confidence are part of having the right psychological make-up. However, they are so important, it is worth distinguishing them from general positivity.

The ideas explained in this book can do for you what a good coach can do – except teach you the specific technical skills of your chosen sport. A coach who understands the principles involved can be more effective; if the learner also understands these principles, coaching is even more effective. It covers everything from basic nutrition and physical training to techniques to effectively learn sporting skills. It then focuses on every aspect necessary to succeed in sport, including:

- Visualisation techniques
- How to get into the zone
- How to alter emotional states
- How to recover from bad experiences

The Champion

- How to unlearn bad habits and technique
- How to increase speed
- How to overcome self-sabotage
- How to stop negative self-talk
- How to prepare for competitions, including training preparation, nutrition and visualisations

The book uses numerous techniques that I have developed and tested with clients and during my own sporting experience. The visualisation techniques discussed in this book have all been tested and are known to be effective and reliable.

Peter D. Campbell

Goal setting and motivation

If you want to succeed you need to know exactly what you want and you need to know how you are going to achieve it. Many people want to be the best in a sport but have little idea how best to train for it. They usually rely on their coaches for guidance and their success largely depends on how good the coach is at teaching technique and planning the student's development. Many coaches are not very good at this and consequently a lot of talent is wasted. Some coaches who have turned out champions are good at working only with a particular personality type. With the right mental equipment, you can take control of your training and use coaches for the information and knowledge they have. If they are good at developing your sporting skills over the long term, you can take advantage of that; if they are only good for teaching basic technical skills, you can learn from them and use this book to help plan your long-term development.

Why are goals important?

Goals motivate you. They are a guide for the path you want to take, assisting decisions related to strategy, and technical approaches that you need to develop in your sporting career. Perhaps you are ambitious, hoping to represent your country or even be one of the best performers in your sport in the world. Your goal might be more modest, but whatever it is, what do you need to do to achieve it?

Goals need to be broken down into elements. Let's assume you want to represent your sport internationally. When do you want to be selected for the national team? To be selected, do you need to be selected for a provincial team? Do you need to win any tournaments? If so, what tournaments do you need to win and when? Or when do you need to be selected for the national team, and how does national selection take place? Once you know the answers to these questions you have a general timeline for the stages in your sporting career development. Once you have these key dates you can build into the time-line dates for the achievement of specific skills that need to be acquired along the way.. You will also need to decide what level of strength and fitness is necessary. Some technical skills will be impossible to perform if you are not strong enough. Similarly, if you are insufficiently fit you might start out well but as you tire, your performance will deteriorate until it can reach the point where you have tunnel- and blurred vision.

To come up with the right goals requires some knowledge of your sport and knowledge of what you need to be good at. A good coach can help you with this if you are starting out in a new sport. If you are already active in a sport you may well have a good idea about what you need to do. Sit down either by yourself or with a coach and set out answers for the questions that are included in following table.

Once you have gone through your goals in detail like this you will have a comprehensive plan for developing your sporting career. While fitness and strength goals might often seem intimidating, if you break them down into stages for the level of fitness you need for each level of performance and slowly work on them, you can develop both strength and fitness without putting undue strain on your body. By being clear about what you need to do to achieve your overall goals you have a benchmark to guide you in training. When you

The Champion

are achieving the smaller goals you will feel motivated because you know that these smaller steps are crucial to achieving your main goal, and this shows you that there is hope in you achieving the overarching goal. This helps to make your goals realistic.

Questions	Example answers: Fencing	Tennis	Soccer/football
What is my overall goal?	Become national champion.	Become national champion.	Be chosen for the national team
What do you need to do to be selected/ to win the championship?	Participate in three national tournaments, getting placings within the top 10 – current season; participate in three national tournaments, getting placings in the top 3 – next season; participate in provincial level competitions, achieve rankings in the top 3 – this season; participate in provincial competitions and win. Third year, win national level competitions and national champs.	Participate in the top tournaments, beat certain individuals, score a certain number of points	Need to improve technical skills, fitness and game strategy to succeed. Talk to the right people and get noticed. (Most sports have intricate politics associated with selection and being aware of these nuances can help selection)
What technical skills do you	Improve all basic elements:	For a tennis player: have a first	Specific ball skills necessary, strike

Peter D. Campbell

need to be able to do well at these tournaments/competitions?	footwork, lunge, attacks; Improve balance; Improve parries, and blade control/accuracy.	serve that is 90% reliable, strong forehand, able to respond well with backhands. Good footwork. Need to be able to respond to fast serves.	accuracy when passing and shooting for goal, specific dribbling skills that are necessary.
What are the key dates for achieving these technical goals?	Improve basic foot work – 2 months; Improve basic lunge – 4 months; Improve parry, lunge and foot combinations – 6 months; Improve accuracy blade control and accuracy.	Revision of basic strokes – 2 months; perfect serve – 4 months; increase speed response;	Focus on developing basic ball skills – 4 months; develop passing accuracy – 2 months; develop long distance passes / goal striking – 6 months; develop on field awareness – 6 months;
Fitness goals – how fit do I need to be for each stage of my career development?	To compete successfully at a provincial level I need a basic fitness of about 8 on the beep test – 1 month of fitness training; To compete well at national level I need to have a fitness of 16 on the beep test. Develop basic fitness of 10 on the beep test – 6 weeks; Increase fitness to 12 on beep test - 3 months; Increase fitness to 14 on beep test - 4 months; Increase fitness to 16 on beep test – 6 months.	Develop basic fitness of 10 on the beep test – 6 weeks; Increase fitness to 12 on beep test - 3 months; Increase fitness to 14 on beep test - 4 months; Increase fitness to 16 on beep test – 6 months.	Develop basic fitness of 10 on the beep test – 6 weeks; Increase fitness to 12 on beep test - 3 months; Increase fitness to 14 on beep test - 4 months; Increase fitness to 16 on beep test – 6 months.

The Champion

| Strength goals? | Leg strength needs to be increased; general strength training followed by plyometric exercises to increase speed and distance of lunges. Increase grip strength for fast blade work, followed by endurance training: strengthen arms and shoulders; To improve general balance, strengthen core muscles and spine; 2 months of general exercises for legs, core and arms, followed by plyometric exercises for legs, and endurance training for shoulders, arms and core. | Develop overall body strength to reduce imbalances and reduce injury risk – 2 months; Develop strength in legs and shoulders- 4 months; develop endurance – 6 months; | Develop overall body strength to reduce imbalances and reduce injury risk – 2 months; Develop strength in legs - 4 months; develop endurance – 6 months; |

Using Goals to motivate you

Having goals that are realistic and progressive is an important part of motivating you to stick with the training regime, devoting time and energy which could be used elsewhere. How we represent and think about our goals makes a difference to whether we try to achieve them. If when thinking about a goal it seems distant, remote, or unachievable; if you have no feelings associated with it, or possibly a feeling of dread, thinking about all the effort that is required to go into achieving it, the chances are you will be unmotivated to achieve it. It is something which sounded good at some stage, but really wasn't worth the commitment.

Think about your goals in a way that is going to motivate you. Much of how we feel, act and behave depends on our visual and special cues. As a general rule humans are attracted by things that are large, shiny, glossy, and colourful and are accessible (nearby). This is the reason why advertisements will often show pictures of products looking shiny and big. Think of the Big Mac which looks absolutely huge in advertisements and often has a red background which is used as a subliminal attempt to stimulate appetite,[1] or the glistening drops on a bottle of coke[2]. So if you want to make your goals more real to you, change the way you represent them to yourself.

---

[1] NASA scientists discovered some time ago that if they painted the inside of their space capsules red, the astronauts ate more, and if they painted them blue, it made them more inclined towards depression. Next time you see food being advertised notice the colours and the presentation of the food and you will start to understand what images affect your subconscious.

[2] A technique used in advertising alcohol as well.

The Champion

Representing your goals:

1. Imagine your goal: perhaps see yourself on the medal podium receiving a gold medal, or perhaps imagine yourself running out onto the field, wearing your national colours for the first time.

2. Notice how far away that image/movie is. Try bringing it closer to you, and notice how your feelings towards it change. Try moving it further away from you, and notice how your feelings change.

3. Now change the colour of the image/movie. If it is colour change it to black and white, if it is in black and white, change it to colour. Notice how that affects the way you feel and relate to the image.

4. Now change the point of view, try experiencing the image in the first person (yourself in the performance role) and in the third person (from the point of view of an observer) and note how it changes the way you feel about the goal and the experience.

5. Now add some sound. Imagine people cheering and clapping. Someone who you admire clapping you on the shoulder and saying, "Well done!"

6. Now add music. Change the tunes, try some rock, or some Beethoven, perhaps a soundtrack from a movie, "Chariots of Fire" or "Gladiator". Notice how these additions change your mood and how you feel about the goal.

7. Having now experimented a little with the representation of the goal, create an image or movie of the goal which really inspires you and makes you feel good. People have their own personal nuances but in general it will probably look something like this: you see the image of yourself on the podium/running onto the field in national colours, the image is larger than life, located in front of you, maybe 20 centimetres or a metre away from you. The image/movie is in vivid colours and is light and is very bright. You can hear a piece of music that you adore and gets your blood pumping.

8. Having imagined this exciting, inspiring image/movie of your goal, really make it memorable by reimagining it several times. The repetition will help cement it in your subconscious mind so that every time you think of your goal it will be this image or movie that you think of. It's easy to do. Think of the exciting and inspiring goal with all the

nuances of location, colour, brightness, and music. After you have enjoyed that image for several seconds, let your mind go blank and then think of something completely different: holiday plans, what you want to eat for dinner, the movie you watched last Friday, anything which will distract your mind for half a minute. Then imagine the exciting, inspiring image/movie again. Repeat the process seven times. The more frequently you do this, the better, but seven times is a good start and is enough to have a positive effect on your motivation and performance.

Once you have done this several times place the image in your future. Imagine being on the precise date when you plan to achieve the goal and experiencing it again, as an event in the future. Then look back into the past and notice everything that you did in order to achieve this goal – in effect, imagine your entire training programme which you went through in order to achieve the goal. Repeat this process seven times as well. What you are doing here is linking all the training to the positive feelings associated with achieving the goal, and by imagining or visualising the training plan you are programming your mind for the execution of the training plan. This is one of the most powerful techniques to motivate you to achieve your success. Goal setting and planning when done right is your key to winning. Let's look at the nuts and bolts of going from plans to reality.

To help maintain motivation while training – **always conclude your training by doing something fun**. This might be an exercise, it might be going out with your training partners for a coffee – but studies show that if you conclude an activity by something which you really enjoy it increases motivation in general and helps sustain you through activities which are less enjoyable.

The Champion

Strength and fitness training

No matter how good your goal setting is, or how resilient you are mentally it is hard to achieve sporting goals without a good level of fitness and strength. While coaches have favourite exercises which they get trainees to do, often there is a lack of information about how fit you need to be, how strong you need to be, and the best approaches for achieving those fitness and strength gains. It is almost assumed that in the process of training for the sport, you will develop the muscles you need. Some sports coaches actively discourage additional training as muscle can been seen as "slowing you down" or as a distraction from technical training. These are often prejudices that are not based on science or come from incorrect applications of training.

Furthermore, there is a lot of information available which is contradictory and misleading. **This section is to give the athlete a few basic**

principles and rules of thumb to work with in order to improve overall sports performance.

While each sport requires the development of specific muscles, sport makes use of the entire body. Consequently you should do complete body training to keep your body strong, and minimise injuries. If you have access to a gym and a trainer, so much the better, and make as much use of both of them as you can. For the rest of us here are the basic principles:

Strength training: do up to 8 repetitions in a set. Some experts recommend that for best strength gains you should keep repetitions below five.

Endurance training: do 15 - 25 repetitions in a set.

Strength and endurance training: Many sports require both strength and endurance. One problem with focusing on strength training is that it can markedly reduce endurance. The way to avoid this problem is to include endurance training as part of your regular training. You can either do a strength set and then an endurance set, or you can spend one day doing strength training and another day doing endurance training. Instead of slowing down training progress it helps to increase it as it provides variety which is helpful. For example, a martial artist might do five clapping press-ups (plyometric training to improve strength and speed) and then follow that by 30 standard press-ups to maintain endurance.

If injured: Physiotherapists often recommend 12 repetitions as a happy medium between building strength and endurance. The muscle produced is larger[3] but it also tends to be filled with liquid, so is not much use to sportspeople. As soon as you have recovered some strength, move onto strength training and then onto endurance training.

Ideal training loads

The following table provides standard recommendations for how to plan training for specific goals. This table is taken from *Foundations in Sports Science*[4] and partially contradicts my other research, however, as the information is recent it is worth mentioning and you can experiment to see what works best for you.

---

[3] The additional bulk comes from the increased size of cells rather than from an increase in their number.

[4] Anthony Bush, *Foundations in Sports Science*, Heinemann Educational Books, 2012

Training load and goals

	Frequency (times per week)	Intensity (% of Max)	Volume	Rest interval
Power	1-2	85-95	1-4 reps 1-2 sets	4-6 min
Strength	3-4	75-85	4-8 reps 3-4 sets	2-3 min
Hypertrophy	4-6	60-80	8-12 reps 5-7 sets	30-90 sec
Endurance	5-7	<60	12-15 reps 5-7 sets	<30 sec

Consistency trumps speed

Ambitious people like to make fast progress. In part this helps reinforce their self-image that they are good at things. In sport it is a mistake. Whether you are learning technique and training to build fitness or strength, consistent training will always trump fast training. Think of your training as a journey, slowly build muscle so you are strong enough to do your sport without injury, slowly learn the techniques and practice them till you perfect them. It is the slow, methodical foundation which will enable you to get to advanced stages in your sport more quickly. Otherwise you risk injuries, and developing incorrect technique which will slow you down and hold you back. Learn to train

The Champion

regularly, consistently and slowly develop your strength, flexibility, stamina and skill.

Developing super muscle

If you need to put on muscle quickly, there is a secret recipe, which was used by the Soviet Special Forces to create killer-looking soldiers. This consisted of doing 10-25 sets of five repetitions with intervals of 3-5 minutes, about three times a week. The muscle gains are apparently extraordinary but the gains in strength are not proportionate to the gain in bulk.[5]

If you lack gym facilities you can get a good all-round work out by doing several bodyweight exercises. If you can get hold of some dumbbells or other weights, incorporating the use of these can be c make a very effective work-out at home.[6]

Exercises

    Push-ups

    Pull-ups

---

[5] Pavel Tsatsouline, *Power to the People!: Russian Strength Training Secrets for Every American,* Dragon Door Publications, 2014.

[6] *The Gymless Body* by Simon Boulter provides plenty of ideas to achieve any training goals at home by increasing muscular resistance.

Full Squats

Sit-ups/leg raises

Dips (tricep dips or parallel dips)

Lifting exercises

Burpies/Star jumps

Skipping/Running

Stretching

Over the course of one to two months, work your way up to doing four sets of 20 for each exercise. Initially take a three to five minute break between each circuit and over time as your strength and fitness grows you will be able to reduce this recovery time. Once you have reached this level of fitness you will be stronger and fitter than most sports people. If you need to reduce the number of repetitions to build strength you can either slow the exercises down (take 10 seconds to lift yourself and 10 seconds to lower yourself; if you need to increase resistance even further you can spend 30 seconds on each lift), reduce the number of limbs you are using (one-hand push-ups instead of two-hand push-ups, one-leg squats instead of two-leg squats), or you can work on developing strength and power by doing

The Champion

plyometric exercises[7] (push-ups with claps, instead of squats do jumps or leaps).

The core: the core is important for improving balance and coordination and is essential for any athlete to develop, exercises such as leg extensions and sit-ups do help develop the core but are problematic, sit-ups, in particular, can cause back injuries and also stooping. The best way to develop core muscles is doing lifting exercises, and exercises holding weights above your head – which is why you see pictures of US marines training by holding huge logs over their heads. It's not because logs are particularly lethal weapons! The other advantage of lifting exercises is that in addition to strengthening the core they also strengthen the back, improve posture, and increase speed.

A basic training plan might look something like this if you are already reasonably strong and exercising three times a week with suitable diet and sleep. Do four circuits of the following exercises:

---

[7] The Oxford English Dictionary defines these as "A form of exercise that involves rapid and repeated stretching and contracting of the muscles, designed to increase strength"

Peter D. Campbell

	Week 1	Week 2	Week 3	Week 4
Push-ups	10	13	16	20
Full squats	10	13	16	20
Pull-ups	3	5	8	10
Sit-ups	10	13	16	20
Dips	10	13	16	20
Lifting exercise	10	13	16	20

Don't let the small numbers fool you, you will be doing four sets of these exercises and they can get tiring if you are doing them regularly. Those who are only at an intermediate or beginner level should start by doing only about five exercises. Beginners may also find it useful to do the exercises only two or three times a week, and stay at the same level for two or three weeks until the body has built up strength and energy levels. Active athletes might find they can start on week four and add a few repetitions every week.

If you are looking for strength gains, take a break of up to five minutes at the end of each circuit to recover. If you want to increase fitness at the same time as doing the callisthenics, reduce the time between circuits. It is recommended that you take a two minute break between circuits, but as you get fitter you will find you can reduce this until eventually, after several weeks training you will be able to do four circuits without a break. If you are already reasonably fit and strong, and such a programme appears to be too simple even on a daily basis, you can alter it to non-stop exercises for ten minutes or fifteen minutes, and increase the number of repetitions. If you want to increase the cardio-load and your muscles are strong enough to do so, do back to back circuit exercises with a high number of repetitions.

When I ran a 22-km half-marathon on bad knees my only exercise had been 13 minutes of non-stop callisthenics a day for a three week period. Doing these exercises can get you fit and strong quickly.

If you want to focus on increasing fitness add either burpies[8] or star-jumps to the circuit.

Depending on the sport you may want to increase the ultimate number of exercises you do for particular muscle groups. In some sports, being strong enough to do 100 push-ups a day may be more than enough, in wrestling it is common for competitors to do 500 push-ups a day. Mike

---

[8] To do a burpy, stand straight, then drop to your hands and knees, extend yourself into a push-up position, lower yourself to the ground, then push explosively up, draw your legs up to your hands in a crouch, and then jump upwards, landing on your feet and standing straight, repeat the process. Do a search on the internet to see pictures and videos of how they are performed if you are in doubt.

Tyson used to do to 500 in addition to his fitness training, sparring and fighting training because push-ups strengthened the specific muscles most needed for a strong punch.

If you need additional training ideas or ways to increase resistance while doing body-weight exercises there are a number of good books on the market: I recommend *The Gymless Body* by Simon Boulter which gives numerous exercises and discusses at length how to increase resistance while training at home or in the park.

Dips

Dips strengthen the arms, shoulders and pectorals and laterals – by adding variations they can also be used to strengthen the abdominal muscles and back muscles. The most common are parallel dips which typically are performed using two horizontal bars. You clasp each bar with your hand and then lower and raise yourself. The parallel bars can be replaced with two chairs or any other objects that are the same height which you can place yourself in between. If this is impossible, you can do tricep dips where you place your hands on an object about 50 centimetres high, with your body facing away from it. Lower yourself so that your body weight is supported by your arms and place your feet about a metre from the object. Then raise and lower yourself, thrusting your hips upwards as you do so. This exercises the arms, the triceps, the quads and the abdominals.

Holds

Although not included in the sample exercise plan, holds are an excellent way of building strength and endurance. The best known of the holds is the bridge or the plank where you hold yourself in a rigid position on your hands and toes. This strengthens the entire body but most fit people can do a bridge for several minutes, which makes it possibly one of the most tedious exercises ever invented. However, this exercise can be made more efficient by placing your hands as far forwards as possible and then contracting your abdominals as if trying to pull your legs and hands together. This becomes difficult to maintain for more than about 10 seconds. Other holds can include simply hanging on a pull up bar; raising yourself on a pull up bar and holding the position; raising yourself on a pull up bar and in the up position then raising your legs to create an L-shape and holding the position. Raising yourself on parallel bars (or your substitution for them) and then thrusting your legs forward to create an L-shape; or thrusting your legs back, to attempt to hold yourself horizontal supported only by your arms (this takes time and practise to achieve).

Lifting exercises

Lifting exercises are perhaps the best way of exercising the entire body and as such are a good way of doing a quick training session. Any weights will do: barbells, dumbbells, kettle bells or homemade improvised weights. These can be made from drink bottles filled with whatever is convenient (water, sand, earth, gravel). You can then use these as individual weights. If you need to increase the weight place them in a bag and lift the bag. There are numerous exercises that can be done with weights from traditional shoulder and arm exercises, to full body lifting exercises. Exercises which are useful can include:

- Full lift from squat, which strengthens arms shoulders and back. Is helpful for straightening stoops that develop from too much computer use. Starting in a squat raise the weight into a position above your head, stand and then squat again.
- Lower back strengthening exercise: hold the weight either close to your chest or with arms extended. Bend at the lower back and then straighten. The exercise

strengthens the lower back, shoulders, arms and abdominals.
- Rotator cuff exercises. If you have weak shoulders or an unstable rotator cuff, you can hold weights in both hands and with straight/extended arms, raise them to shoulder height. In order to strengthen all muscles equally you should do exercises raising the arms forwards in front of you; laterally, with your arms going upwards from your side to create a T-shape; and also laterally again, but this time with your arms turned so that the forearms are facing forwards, not on top.
- You can also place weights in a backpack and run with them if you need it increase resistance training when running.

Running

A lot of people don't like running. One of the main problems is that when we start training we often run too fast, winding ourselves and feeling like death. Furthermore, running causes a lot of injuries, so that aerobic workouts doing body weight exercises might seem preferable. However, running can be pleasurable and a high level of fitness can be acquired without pain.

Peter D. Campbell

There is increasing scientific evidence and a lot of anecdotal evidence indicating that expensive running shoes cause injuries.[9] Stanford University head running coach Vin Lananna recommends that runners train in the cheapest shoes they can find..[10] If you are starting out running, start off slowly for the first couple of weeks until your body has adjusted to the movements. Go for short runs, about 15-20 minutes, then start intensity training. This is most easily done if you have some way of monitoring your speed, either a treadmill or a smartphone with a running app. Start running at a slow easy speed, perhaps 8 or 9 km/h. After a couple of minutes increase the speed to about 12 km/h and maintain it for a minute, before dropping back to your initial speed, which you maintain for two or three minutes and then increase it again. To help you judge the speed, at 8 km/hour you should be able to carry on a conversation with your running partner (if you have one, otherwise you can always start talking to yourself). At 12 km/h you would be able to talk only in a staccato fashion between gulps of air. Over the course of several

---

[9]Christopher McDougall, *Born to Run*, Profile Books, 2010. McDougall discusses this point in detail in Chapter 25.

[10] Ibid. p. 172.

weeks increase the base speed and the higher speeds. Within a month or two you should be able to increase your base running speed to about 16 km/h. Top marathon runners run entire marathons at 20 km/h, so you will be a little slower compared to marathoners, but for most fitness purposes you will be pretty fit. To develop this level of fitness you only need to run 2-3 km every couple of days for a few weeks. On off-days you could perhaps go for long, slow jogs or brisk walks to help ease any stiffness from your body. View Appendix 1 for a detailed running plan if you are interested in taking running seriously.

If you want to increase resistance while running you can try running on sand or load a backpack with weights and run with those. Don't overdo the weights or the running. These can cause injury, but they do have additional benefits in that <u>in moderation</u> they strengthen the joints, tendons and ligaments. Being attentive to how your body is responding can help you avoid over-use injuries.

The Beep test

An easy way of measuring your fitness is to use the beep test. You can download audio files of the beep test online (search "beep test mp3 free download"). The test requires that you run between two points 20 metres apart between beeps. The interval between beeps decreases, forcing you to run faster to the point that you can no longer keep up. By doing regular beep tests you can keep track of your increasing fitness and this helps you maintain motivation. As the beep test is also used by sports organisations, police and military, you have the opportunity to compare yourself with others and compliment yourself on not only being fitter than the majority of the population but also the majority of police officers or soldiers, etc. Just don't rub it in their faces unless you are certain you can run faster!

The Cooper Test and VO_2 Max

Another good way of testing your fitness and keeping track of your progress is the Cooper Test. In this test you run as fast as you can for 12 minutes and measure the distance covered. This race against yourself can be used as a simple comparison, but it can also be used to calculate a measurement called the VO_2 Max which is your maximum oxygen uptake. The fitter you are, the faster you can run and the higher your oxygen uptake. Although age and sex affect your VO_2 Max, if you are a competitive sportsperson you will probably want to be getting scores in the 50s or 60s. Olympic class athletes have scores ranging from the high 70s to the low 90s (extremely rare).

The Champion

The VO² Max can also be calculated based on your beep test results. All these calculations can be easily found and done on the internet. Try search strings such as "vo2 max beep test calculator" or "cooper test vo2 calculator".

Those who want to calculate their VO_2 Max independently can do so using the following formula:

VO_2 max = 33.3 + (Distance in metres ÷ Time in minutes − 133) × 0.172

For example, your daily run might be two miles around the local park in 11 minutes 30 seconds to run. Your VO_2 max would be: 33.3 + (3200 ÷ 11.5 − 133) × 0.172 = 58.28.

Fitness results can be compared on the following tables:

Vo₂ Max fitness tables

Men

Age	Low	Fair	Average	Good	High	Athletic	Elite
20-29	<38	39-43	44-51	52-56	57-62	63-69	70+
30-39	<34	35-39	40-47	48-51	52-57	58-64	65+
40-49	<30	31-35	36-43	44-47	48-53	54-60	61+
50-59	<25	26-31	32-39	40-43	44-48	49-55	56+
60-69	<21	22-26	27-35	36-39	40-44	45-49	50+

Women

Age	Low	Fair	Average	Good	High	Athletic	Elite
20-29	<28	29-34	35-43	44-48	49-53	54-59	60+
30-39	<27	28-33	34-41	42-47	48-52	53-58	59+
40-49	<25	26-31	32-40	41-45	46-50	51-56	57+
50-65	<21	22-28	29-36	37-41	42-45	46-50	50+
65 +	<18	19-24	25-32	33-37	38-41	42-46	47+

Skipping

If you suffer from shin-splints or other such injuries that blight would-be runners, or simply have nowhere to run, you might try skipping. This is often considered to be as good as or better than running, although you might have slightly less control over intensity. Complete your workout with a 10-15 minute skip.

The "train-to–fatigue" controversy

Most trainers advise you to train to fatigue. That is, we are told, breaking the muscle fibres which regenerate to be stronger than before. This is familiar to you as muscle stiffness after unaccustomed exercise. This is advice I have followed all of my life and I do get a sense of satisfaction from the weary feeling that comes with muscles having been worked to exhaustion in a heavy weight-training session. However,

The Champion

Pavel Tsatsouline who was involved in training Soviet Special Forces and now is a consultant to the US Navy Seals recommends against training to fatigue, claiming that it simply takes athletes longer to recover. He observes that strong-men who made their living by feats of astonishing strength in the 19th and early 20th centuries refused to train to fatigue claiming that it left them tired, not invigorated and was ineffective.[11] I recommend that you experiment and find out which approach seems to get the best results for you.

Advantages of training to fatigue

While training to fatigue might slow down strength gains (see above) there are important reasons for athletes to occasionally train to fatigue and beyond. During competitions and tournaments you will be giving it everything you've got. At some stage you will hit the wall. This happens when your muscles run out of carbohydrates and your body starts using fat. Using fat requires the transformation of fat into carbohydrate, a process which requires energy. At this stage you can still function but it requires

---

[11] Pavel Tsatsouline, *Power to the People!: Russian Strength Training Secrets for Every American*, Dragon Door Publications, 2014.

increasing effort to stay focused. To avoid this, athletes will often drink energy drinks, eat sugar products and chocolate. However, as a high performing athlete your body should be accustomed to performing well when approaching exhaustion and the only way to learn to perform well when exhausted, is by training to exhaustion and then continue training.[12] This is not something for beginners or intermediate sportspeople to do because when you are tired it is much harder to perform with good technique. Consequently training when tired can be a good way to learn bad habits and develop bad technique. When you train in an exhausted state, make sure you focus on doing it correctly. A good way to develop skills at exhaustion is to do high intensity training, interval running until you can go no further and

---

[12] Interestingly enough, it is possible to train your body to exercise using only fat reserves, and in this way avoid "hitting the wall". The technique is fully described in Chapter 32 of Christopher McDougall's book *Natural Born Heroes*. In essence, change your diet to food using only low glycogen index carbohydrates (basically no sugars or heavily processed food), then train keeping your pulse beneath x (where x = 180 minus your age). When your pulse increases beyond this level, your brain needs the energy that comes from high glycogen index foods (sugars) and the body starts burning these. Maintain a low pulse and get fit enough to be able to maintain a low pulse throughout competition and you will be able to power yourself on fat alone, claims McDougall. It is known as the Maffetone Method.

then move onto technical training. Once you have developed good technique when exhausted you can then move onto competitive training at exhaustion.

Rest and constant training

Rest is as important as training. 'Over training' leads to weakness, overall fatigue and injuries. If you need a day or two to recover from training, take it. Muscles need to rebuild. However, if you find that muscle recovery is taking excessively long – more than four or five days, look at your diet: are you getting enough protein or enough carbohydrates? Another possible explanation is that you may need to add vitamins or minerals to your diet.

One way of enable ongoing training is to vary the type if training from day to day. For example, do weight training one day, and running the next. As most athletes will be doing sport specific training as well, it is important that such ongoing training does not tire. Ideally you want to build up strength and endurance in the off-season so that you have the capacity to support sport specific training in season without pushing your body to the limit. Muscle retains its strength for about two weeks of inactivity – which means that if you are having trouble with muscle recovery or illness you don't need to train everyday. Furthermore, body-builders and weightlifters claim that for building muscle you need to train only once or twice a week. These claims are supported by much of what Tim Ferriss claims in his book *The Four Hour Body.* However, as stated earlier Pavel Tsatsouline provides compelling arguments in his books never to train to fatigue, but train frequently. So an exhausting training session which leaves your muscles bruised and painful for two to three days, would be replaced with short, intense training sessions which stop short of fatigue. This means you can train frequently. Such an approach means that you can throw in a few exercises as part of your daily routine. A few push-ups before meals, a couple of pull-ups whenever you enter your bedroom etc. This means strength training can be fitted seamlessly into your day, building strength without ever having to go to the limit of your strength. This should give you more energy and barely take up any noticeable time from your day. For example if you want to improve the number of push-ups you do, instead of doing 30 press-ups to failure, by doing 15 press-ups several times a day, you will increase your ability to do more press-ups, without ever having to push the muscle to its limit. This is a gentle form of training which doesn't stress the body as much, is easier

The Champion

to fit into your day and as it doesn't tire or hurt, you will find yourself more motivated to do it. Doing half your maximum is a good way to develop to exercise.

Peter D. Campbell

Diet and nutrition

Most trainers now recommend a so-called palaeolithic diet. The truth of the matter is that our paleo ancestors did not eat paleo diets, they ate what they could get which depended on where they were living. However, the neo-palaeoliths may be onto something. A large number of illnesses which blight the modern world seem to be caused by processed food. Get rid of the processed food, eat meat, lentils, nuts, beans, fruits, rice and potatoes if you need additional calories. Milk is a good source of protein and calcium but is becoming unpopular. Our paleo-ancestors didn't consume it and modern processing in the interests of public health makes 'whole food' devotees suspicious. The key point about diet is to get plenty of protein and have plenty of greens. An adult male in training needs about 1.6-1.8 grams of protein for every kilogram of body weight. Women need 15% less protein. Lean meat has about 30 grams

The Champion

of protein per 100 grams of meat, milk has about 3 grams of protein per 100 mls. Charts for protein counting can be found in Appendix 2.

While most sports books emphasise the need for protein to build muscle, energy is equally important. Energy is contained in protein, carbohydrate and fat. It is most often represented as calories or kilojoules. In terms of carbohydrates, depending on the form of exercise and the duration of exercise you will need to consume between 5 and 10 grams of carbohydrates per kilogram of body weight. Full details can be seen in tables included in the appendices to this book.

An athlete in training needs anything from 2,500 to 4,000 calories a day. Olympian Michael Phelps when training for the Olympics was said to be using 12,000 calories a day,[13] Navy Seals in training can burn over 7,000 calories a day. There are plenty of sites on the internet which calculate the number of calories needed depending on the type and amount of exercise. Just search "how many calories do I need in a day". Other searches can be for "Basal Metabolic Rate Calculator" or simply "BMR calculator" but these then require

---

[13] This figure is much cited, including by Tim Ferriss in *The Four Hour Body*. It has subsequently been debunked.

Peter D. Campbell

additional calculations to determine how many calories you need.[14]

The following table will give you some idea of how much you will need to eat.

Calories per day

Height (cm)	Light Activity	Moderate Activity	Heavy activity
150	1455-1920	1649-2176	1940-2560
155	1560-2040	1768-2312	2080-2720
160	1650-2175	1870-2465	2200-2900
165	1770-2325	2006-2635	2360-3100
170	1875-2460	2125-2788	2500-3280
175	1980-2610	2244-2958	2640-3480
180	2100-2760	2380-3128	2800-3680
185	2220-2910	2516-3298	2960-3880

To calculate how much you should be eating look at the table. For example: a 75 kg male, 175 centimetres tall, doing moderate exercise once a day or once every two days (about an hour of exercise) would need 2244-2958 calories a day

---

[14] A basic formula for calculating basal metabolic rate is (bodyweight in kg x 22) + (4 x bodyweight) or (bodyweight in pounds x 10) + (2 x bodyweight).

The Champion

He will need 120 grams of protein a day, and 525 grams of carbohydrates (seven grams of carbohydrates per kilogram of bodyweight – see Appendix 2). Both protein and carbohydrates provide four calories each, so (120 g protein + 525 g carbohydrates) x 4 = 2580 calories. Your body also needs fat. If you have 30 grams of fat (one gram of fat is eight calories) that will create another 240 calories. In total he will have a planned consumption of 2820 calories.

Count the protein, carbohydrates and fat of everything you eat for a couple of days until you have a fairly good idea of how much items are worth and then maintain a running average to keep up the required amount. Monitor the results, if you are putting on fat, increase the exercise or decrease the consumption. If you have slow muscle recovery increase protein and carbohydrate consumption.

Full tables for calculating consumption and energy needs can be found in Appendix 2.

To recover from training, eat a gram of carbohydrate for every kilogram you weigh within 15-20 minutes. Examples of recovery snacks can be seen in Appendix 2.

Peter D. Campbell

How to train for your sport

Learning new skills

We generally perform better when we are relaxed; we also learn better. Before starting any training session spend five minutes relaxing. Sit down by yourself and practise what is known in the police and military as "tactical breathing". Breathing is done through your nose. Breathe in to a count of four, hold it in for a count of four, then breath out to a count of four, stay empty for a count of four and then repeat the process all over again. When breathing, breathe into your diaphragm not your lungs. This breathing is beneficial in that it helps you to relax, it also brings in additional oxygen and increases energy availability. This is a technique which has been used by athletes now for many years, and over the past ten years it has gained popularity among elite military units as well. Navy SEALS swear by it[15].

When you have finished tactical breathing, visualise the training session that you are about to begin. Often when training with a coach I am unaware of what will happen precisely in training so I focus on what I know, executing basic techniques well, being relaxed throughout the training and able to perform well against my opponents. I visualise myself being aware and able to respond to a range of situations. Visualisation will be discussed in greater detail below.

When learning a new skill

1. Have it demonstrated several times, focusing initially on the key elements (grip, movement, balance, etc.), and then gradually move onto the finer elements that need to be done correctly too.

2. After you know how the technique is performed, envisage performing it several times. This is a process which should already have begun when watching the demonstrations. For this reason I like to see a demonstration a total of

---

[15] Cole Tucker, *Killer Athletes: America's Special Operations Warriors Share Lessons & Advice To Help Young Athletes Become Champions!*, CreateSpace Independent Publishing Platform, 2014

seven times. In Loren Christensen's book on mental rehearsal he describes how he learnt to perform a perfect kata by doing only mental rehearsal.[16] The advantage of rehearsing skills mentally in advance is that you have no physical limitations, therefore you are less likely to make errors, and consequently are less likely to learn something incorrectly.

3. Once you have mentally rehearsed the action several times, physically go through the action slowly, focusing on getting it right. If you learn a skill right the first time, you won't have to correct it in the future. Start off slowly, rehearsing it in slow motion several times until you are confident that everything is correct and then increase the speed. Once you are certain that you are doing it correctly. There is no need to rush things. Focus on getting it right. This is especially important for learning basic techniques that are the foundation for advanced skills. If you can't walk properly, running is difficult.

4. Once you can perform a certain skill well you need to develop using it in different circumstances: increase speed, practice it under stress. Increase your heart rate to 145 and

---

[16] Loren W. Christensen, *Mental Rehearsal for Warriors: For Cops, Soldiers and Martial Artists*, 2014

The Champion

practice it then. Increase your heart rate to 175 and practice it again. If you can perform well in such conditions – then you can consider the skill mastered.

The process of learning, thinking things out in your head before you do them might seem unnecessarily slow, but it is the best way to ensure that you master a skill quickly. This process I developed from using accelerated learning principles and then successfully applied them to sport. However, I was interested to find when researching this book that the US Marine Corps use a similar, very supportive approach to teach marines to shoot. So does the Australian Army, which even starts soldiers off on a simulator to ensure they learn to shoot properly before graduating to real weapons.

Once you have learnt a skill well, you then need to learn to apply it in real conditions. This is important because memories are linked to the neural networks that were operating at the time you learnt a skill. For example, if you learn a martial arts move in a relaxed environment, the chemical cocktail in your body will be quite different from when you are attacked on the street. If this happens to you, your system will be charged with adrenalin, cortisol and testosterone. This is one reason why people can freeze with mind blanks in stressful situations: the chemical balance in their body is so different from what they are accustomed to, that a whole range of neural networks are simply non-functional.[17]

General training

A general training session should similarly start with tactical breathing and be followed up with visualisation. Before practicing old skills or competing, go for a run or do shuttle sprints to raise your pulse to 145. This is important as the human body functions optimally at a pulse of 115 to 145. If you are training below or above this limit your training will be less successful. It is for this reason that if you start competing cold you perform significantly worse than if you have had a warm up.

 Go through your training. If you play a game like golf, before striking the ball visualise or imagine exactly what you will do in order to play the perfect stroke. If you play a sport like tennis, you can do the same thing before serving.[18] For sports in which you have less time to visualise such as

---

[17] This also potentially explains so called repressed memories that only come back to an individual during extreme fear.

[18] See the section on *Unlearning bad habits* page 114.

The Champion

martial arts, perform visualisation before a bout or combat and support this with anchoring techniques (see section on *Anchoring*, page 86).

Some coaches like to accustom trainees to performing under stress by shouting and bullying during training. While there might be a place for this in preparing athletes, it is often overused and I know of several cases involving martial arts where it has dramatically slowed people's progress as well as reducing the joy of training. The training environment should be supportive and comfortable, enabling sportspeople to focus on improving performance.

At the end of any training session, conclude it with stretching, this not only helps prevent injury and soreness after exercise but also helps build muscle.[19]

You can complete your training by carrying out tactical breathing and doing a review using visualisation. Visualisation can be used as a review of what you did well and can also be used to distance yourself from anything that was not well done during training. (see *Visualisation and*

---

[19] Pavel Tsatsouline, *Power to the People!: Russian Strength Training Secrets for Every American*, Dragon Door Publications, 2014.

mental rehearsal, page 78). Then fill out your training diary.

Prototype training session

1. Relaxation (tactical breathing)
2. Visualisation
3. Running (increase pulse to 145)
4. Training session
5. Stretching
6. Visualisation (review)
7. Conclude training by doing something enjoyable.

Visualisation and mental rehearsal

Visualisation is one of these terms which has become increasingly in vogue over the last 15 years and is often suggested as the be-all and end-all solution for any problems (along with "being positive"). However, most people seem to be unaware how it works, why it works or how to use it. Put simply, visualisation is mental rehearsal and the concept has been around for at least the last hundred years, while humans have probably used it since the beginning of time to prepare for ordeals. There are numerous variations of visualisation and different representations you can use to achieve different results.

The term 'visualisation' is a misnomer, because when done properly it doesn't include only visual imagery but also sounds, feelings and sensations. The purpose of a visualisation is to create as much of the feel of reality as you possibly can.

This is a skill and often requires concentration and persistence to develop. People who are largely visual may have trouble stepping into a visualisation to feel sensations, people who are intellectual might find it hard to see images. The point is to do it; it doesn't matter if it isn't perfect; you have plenty of time to perfect it and it will nonetheless be beneficial to you.

How it works

Visualisation is one way of transferring thoughts and instructions to your subconscious. The subconscious responds to these images and ideas as if they are real. You will have noticed this from time to time when, for example, you are thinking of something that makes you anxious you notice that your hands begin to sweat and your pulse increases. Similarly, by thinking in detail about how we want to perform, we are essentially rehearsing the process of high performance. This is laying the ground work to achieve things that you want to achieve. It establishes and strengthens neural networks in your brain and fires neurons throughout your body, simulating the task, and then strengthens those neural networks. The stronger the neural network, the better it is at performing the specific task. If you have established a neural network where you are performing a task correctly, then repeating the visualisation of that task is almost as beneficial as the task itself. Some of the earliest research in visualisation was undertaken by Australian psychologist Alan Richardson in an experiment in which he separated volunteers into three groups. All three groups were taught to throw a basketball into a basketball hoop. Over a period of 20 days one group had regular practice, the second group performed only visualisations, and the third group did nothing at all. When the groups were retested, the first group which had practised scored the best results with an improvement of 24%, the second group which did only visualisations achieved a 23% improvement. The control group that didn't practise, didn't improve at all.[20]

Visualisation can be used to increase training hours without putting the same stress on your body. This means that you can train more, or if you have no access to facilities, you can still practice your sport. It isn't as good as real training, but it is almost as good. This means that if you are commuting to work, trapped in traffic, waiting in a queue, etc., you can put in some more

---

[20] Alan Richardson, "Mental Practice: A Review and Discussion", *Research Quarterly*, American Association for Health, Physical Education and Recreation Volume 38, Issue 1, 1967.

practice refining your golf drive, your baseball pitch or your kata.

However, visualisation is more than a replacement for hard work at the gym: it is a way of priming the neural networks you want to use and instructing your brain what you really want to do. This is why visualisation before your strike, your drive or your putt on the golf green is important, it's why tennis players take so long over their serves – they are visualising exactly how they are going to serve and respond to the return.

Ways to visualise

There are two main ways of visualising. One is 'associated visualisation' in which you experience the event through your own eyes and feel it in your body. The other is to visualise an experience in the third person ('dissociated visualisation') so that you see yourself performing the action as if another person were watching you. A survey of US navy seals indicated that they fall into three groups when it comes to visualisation, those that associate, those that dissociate, and those that do both. There seemed to be little difference in performance between the different methods.[21]

These results are a little misleading, however, as there is significantly more to visualisation than mental rehearsal. ***How*** you mentally rehearse an experience alters how your subconscious thinks of it. Mental rehearsal primes the way you subconsciously perceive and respond to experiences. Mental rehearsal can and is used in various forms of therapy to help people recover from post traumatic stress disorder (PTSD) and a range of other psychological issues. Therefore, the way you visualise your training can dramatically alter the results of the visualisation.

Basic visualisation

In its simplest form, visualisation is little different from a very realistic day-dream or fantasy about your sport. Imagine the technique you want to improve, or the bout that you are going to fight; imagine what you see, what you can hear, what you feel. Become as aware of all of these things as possible.

If you are visualising a shot at goal as a soccer or rugby player, see the ball in front of you, the goal

---

[21] Loren W. Christensen, *Mental Rehearsal for Warriors: For Cops, Soldiers and Martial Artists*, 2014

posts just ahead of you, become aware of the sound of the crowd, or the silence of the spectators as they wait in expectation; notice your pulse, the sensations in your legs as you are about to move. Then you feel yourself approach the ball, your legs move, you feel how you strike the ball with your foot, and see the strike and as you feel your body following through with the kick, your eyes follow the ball as it passes through the goal posts.

You might find that you naturally want to watch yourself shoot for goal from a dissociated position. Try it both ways on a training field and notice if it makes a difference. If it does, use the method which is most effective for you. However, as a general guide, the closer the image is to you, the more you experience the mental rehearsal and the larger you make it, the more effective it will be.

If you are a goal keeper you will want to mentally rehearse an attack and your response to it, and see yourself blocking the ball.

If you do martial arts mentally rehearse strikes, blocks and parries. Mentally rehearse series of movements so they flow into one another. Feel all the movements in your muscles, notice your footwork.

The Champion

For those playing field sports such as rugby, soccer and hockey, you can visualise such moments as receiving a pass, taking the ball forwards, avoiding tackles, and passing it on, or taking it all the way to goal and shooting, or scoring a try. In sports such rowing and running you can visualise specific parts of the race, getting off to a good start, overtaking the leader, the final sprint towards the end, etc. But in doing this don't just be thinking passively about the activities: put yourself mentally in the same state as you would be as if actually performing.

If you are engaged in a physical training session you can perform visualisation in advance, seeing yourself doing well throughout the training, enjoying it and achieving the training goals for the day. This is something that we often do unaware as we anticipate an event. If we are looking forward to an event we think about the positive elements which we want to enjoy; if we dread the event we focus on the negative elements which we do not want to endure. Think of social events that you have wanted to attend or have wanted to avoid, think of training sessions that you have wanted to attend and those you have wanted to avoid. The images we create in our minds when considering these events either cause our antipathy, or are used to justify it. Take control of your thoughts: if you are not looking forward to a training, check what images you are associating with it, and consciously change them to positive ones. *By having defeatist thoughts, you are priming yourself for a defeatist experience;* it might surprise you, but you are more likely to have an unsatisfactory experience if you have been thinking negatively about it in advance.

You can also use visualisation during training itself. Christensen in his book *Mental Rehearsal for Warriors* mentions a case when a policeman who was also a body builder sustained an injury while making an arrest. He was reduced to training with weights of only a couple of pounds when he had previously been using 80-90 pound weights. As he performed these exercises using two-pound dumbbells he imagined that he was still lifting heavy weights, recalling the feel of the steel grips in his hands, the way the weights strained his muscles, the appearance of his chest and the sound of the gym. By the time he had progressed to 5-pounders, he was shocked to discover that he had achieved increased muscle mass.

Advanced visualization techniques are discussed at length following the next chapter on anchoring.

The Champion

Anchoring: Getting into the flow and emotional control

While many think that visualisation is the crux of sports psychology, it is only one of several techniques that can be used to improve sporting performance. One of the most important elements for developing emotional control and focus during competition is anchoring. Throughout a competition as your success fluctuates you are subject to mood changes: frustration, anger, joy, hope, doubt, exhaustion and fear. I remember in some competitions being hit by such a strong rush of adrenalin that I have lost control of the fine motor skills necessary to hit exposed areas of my opponent when fencing. Being able to control these changes in your emotions is critical to being resilient and being able to perform.

Anchoring is a technique which gives you control over your emotions. Anchoring is based on the concept of classic conditioning discovered by Dr Pavlov at the beginning of the 20th century and who is known largely from reference to "Pavlov's Dog". Pavlov's discovery was that subconscious behaviour could be triggered by association and that such associations could be deliberately created by conditioning. In the case of Pavlov's dogs, the dogs were conditioned to salivate when a bell was rung by providing food simultaneously with ringing the bell. This discovery has become one of the cornerstones of modern advertising whereby favourable associations are deliberately linked to a product or brand, it is also used extensively in sport and military training to develop automatic responses.

The most common experience people have which is an example of anchoring is when walking down a street or sitting in a café and hearing a once-familiar song. Often the song triggers a series of associations and memories – the time when you first heard it, where you were, who you were with, etc. This is an anchor which was subconsciously established connecting the memories and good feelings you were experiencing at the time, with the music you heard. This is one reason why people often listen throughout their lives to the same music they heard when they were children or teenagers.

The Champion

Another common anchor is associated with close friends or lovers. When you see them, your mood suddenly changes and you forget everything else. It is interesting that with lovers while the relationship is going well they establish positive anchors, but when the relationship has deteriorated they establish negative anchors, so that they only need to hear a particular tone of voice or see a particular expression to be swept back into the previous mood or circumstances.

Emotions, feelings and states of mind can be associated with various anchors of which the triggers might be sounds, images or physical contact. For developing sporting skills it is useful to establish physical anchors that you can apply before and during a match, game or competition.

There are three common states of mind athletes want to be in before and during a competition:

1. Calm – relaxed, observant, ready to respond;
2. Flow – that state where you are performing at your best and you aren't really consciously aware of what you are doing, your timing is perfect, everything flows smoothly;

3. Alert – particularly common in martial arts when you need a lot of adrenaline and energy.

Installing anchors

Step 1: To install an anchor firstly you need to decide what action you want to use as the trigger. This needs to be an action that you can easily perform while doing your sport. For sport I have a range of anchors which I can use with my left hand and consist of holding my fingers in set, unnatural positions(so I don't use the anchors accidentally). I have trained divers who have chosen to use the "All OK" sign as a trigger to relax them. I worked with one corporate executive who chose to hold his wrist in a certain way, which he could do inconspicuously at meetings, to control nervousness (and sometimes anger). Other sportspeople I have worked with have used triggers such as holding an ear between their thumb and forefinger. I had a client who had subconsciously set up an anchor by stroking his hair. Choose an appropriate trigger for yourself appropriate to the demands of your sport. Maintaining various holds, or applying pressure to particular parts of the body work best as they give the body time to adjust to the physiological changes that need to take place.

The Champion

Step 2: Decide on the state you want to anchor. Athletes usually choose to create separate anchors for each state they want to use when competing. A state of calm is often used before a bout, fight, penalty shot, etc. to enable the sportsperson to focus on the current task and take control of nerves, fear, or excess energy. A state of flow is usually triggered after the athlete has achieved calmness, and is used to place him/her in that state in which performance comes easily and comfortably. A 'psyched–up' or alert state is usually only useful if you are going to do something that requires large release of physical energy. Weight lifters might want to psyche themselves up before a big lift; boxers and martial artists will want to psyche themselves up for particularly aggressive opponents. I have personally only deliberately psyched myself up once for an epée bout and that was against an opponent who was more aggressive than I, and who was accustomed to being the most aggressive person on the piste. I wanted to turn the tables on him and needed to psych myself up, to force him to fight on my terms not his. For most sports being calm or in flow is a more productive state. However, psyching can be used if you are underperforming because you are not getting an adrenaline rush.

Step 3: Go into the state you want to anchor. This is achieved by remembering a time when you felt the desired state. Remember the experience in careful detail, remember what was happening, remember what you were doing, what you did, remember how you felt, remember what you heard, what you saw and cast yourself back into that experience.

Step 4: Apply the trigger. Once you feel that you are fully re-living the experience, apply the trigger which you have already decided on. While continuing to apply the trigger, continue also to experience the state which you want to anchor. Hold this for about 30 seconds to a minute. By establishing a unique trigger when you are in the desired state you create an association between the trigger and the state, so that in the future, when you use the trigger, it triggers the state – just like Pavlov's dogs salivating when they heard the bell.

Step 5: Strengthening the anchor. Once is enough to establish an anchor, but it never hurts to practice it. Deliberately apply the anchor several times a day and while applying it go through the entire process described in step 3. When you are naturally in the desired state, apply the trigger again, just to strengthen the association.

Anchoring is a powerful technique, and is often something which can be done in a few minutes. When giving demonstrations to athletes, or asked at a dinner party for a tip to improve sports performance, I usually teach anchoring. However, it is not always easy to go into the necessary state. For example some sportspeople might have had only a few fleeting experiences of being "in flow" so recreating that state can be difficult. It is something that might need practice and effort to achieve. If you cannot get into the state of flow, keep on trying, but establish anchors for being relaxed and ready, rather than in flow. The flow will come with time.

To create an anchor

1. Choose the trigger
2. Choose the state you want to anchor
3. Go into the desired state
4. Activate the trigger
5. Strengthen the anchor

Using anchors

I was once working with a photographer who was frequently diving at a particularly dangerous site on the New Zealand coast. The location was so difficult and dangerous to access that no-one ever dived there and consequently the environment was almost pristine. Entering and leaving the location required swimming through channels of rocks which funnelled the tide the force of which could easily sweep a diver against the rocks.

In an effort to develop the photographer's professional work I taught him about anchors and he applied an anchor for calmness. Sometime later he was diving at the dangerous site and while he was underwater the weather changed and he, with his team, surfaced at the entrance of the channel to find himself in the middle of a storm. Seeing that entering the channel was too dangerous to attempt, he did the only thing that any normal person would do – he froze. His mind went blank and for crucial seconds on the surface he did not know how to respond, the only thing he recognised was that he needed to be calm to take control of the situation. Never having believed that the anchor worked, he tried it. Almost immediately his mind cleared. He recognised that the greatest risk was while they were on the surface. He immediately took his team underwater and then swam further down the coast to another location which although covered in rocks was significantly less dangerous than the usual entry and exit point. The entire team, with help from the shore crew, managed to

The Champion

leave the water without incident. The safe conclusion to the dive was largely due to the photographer's ability to control his state and remain calm when others might have panicked. Anchoring is a technique that you can use in numerous situations to retain mastery over your emotions and consequently events.

In sporting competitions anchoring can be used in pre-tournament preparation: it can also be used between games/bouts, and also before points. In tennis, for example, it is possible to use an anchor before each serve; in martial arts, before each round or just after each point. In team sports such as soccer, hockey and rugby, it can be used before the game and sometimes before penalties, depending on the time restraints.

How anchors can help you

Throughout a fight/bout/game/tournament your emotional state changes. If you feel confident that you are going to win you can become careless in your performance; if you are exhilarated by your success you might get an additional shot of adrenalin which can give you the shakes. Similarly if you have been given a shock – your opponent has just raced into an unexpected lead, and you feel that everything is lost – your performance can deteriorate. By using an anchor you can sharpen your focus and psychological resilience states of mind that are critical for maintaining high performance while competing.

The Champion

Develop resilience

Martin Seligman, one of the world's leading experts on depression and positive psychology, conducted a number of interesting (if not very friendly) experiments on man's best friend – the faithful canine. He placed dogs in a cage and passed an electric shock through the cage's floor at random intervals. Initially the dogs jumped, yelped and scratched at the door to try to escape the shocks, but after a while they became apathetic and made no effort to escape the shocks. Once a dog had become apathetic it would not even try to escape when an escape was provided but would lie on the ground and receive the shocks as they were delivered. Seligman termed this condition 'learned helplessness'.[22]

---

[22] Lt. Col. Dave Grossman, "Chapter 5", *On Killing*, Open Road Media; Revised edition, 1 April 2014.

Other dogs were given shocks but before they became apathetic they would be given an escape, which they took. These dogs became inoculated against learned helplessness and would then be able tolerate more shocks than the initial group without becoming resigned to the situation.

What Seligman discovered is what drill sergeants and physical trainers have been doing as second nature for centuries and can be referred to as "hardening up". By placing high levels of stress on people and then relenting, people become resilient to stress – they become tempered. With a good coach sportspeople can be trained to withstand higher levels of pressure, maintaining focus and form. Such training is most often done with physical training that helps build endurance and resilience to fatigue. However, this is less useful for building <u>emotional</u> resilience which is needed when a sportspeople have suffered a demoralising defeat or set-back during an event, and need to pull themselves together to re-establish a competitive focus to continue in the game or competition. Most coaches and trainers refer to this ability as a matter of experience – once you have been in a situation enough times, you toughen up, learn to pull yourself together. However, there are a number of techniques that can be used to help you pull yourself together.

The Champion

Becoming a Navy SEAL

The US Navy SEALs choose individuals who are psychologically resilient, intelligent and physically fit, and then put them through a gruelling six week selection course called BUDS. Successful finishers of the course would then go onto further training before finally joining an active SEAL unit. Despite the high level of candidates that were chosen to undertake selection, only 24% of candidates successfully complete the training programme. The navy wanted to increase the candidates' success rate and hired psychologist Eric Potterat to look at strengthening mental resilience. Potterat devised a four-step process to increase recruit resilience. By applying these four steps the navy increased their graduation rate by 50%.[23]

---

[23] Tom Dotz, Tom Hoobyar, Susan Sanders, "Chapter 3: Living in the Zone", *NLP: The Essential Guide to Neuro-Linguistic Programming*, William Morrow Paperbacks, 2013.

Peter D. Campbell

Potterat's formula for resilience

1. Focus on the present
2. Imagine how good it will feel when you have completed the activity
3. Breathe deeply
4. Cheer yourself on

During competition it is easy to become distracted. "If I win this bout, I will have to fight Thomas … the chances are 50:50 but if I beat him I'm into the semis and should be against Bill, and I know I can beat Bill hands down. That means I'll be into the finals with a chance for a gold and I'm a dead cert for a silver." While these thoughts are going on, you are distracted from the current bout and instead of defeating Thomas, you lose the current bout because you weren't paying enough attention to your opponent.

Similarly if you are losing a fight, or your team is losing, it is easy to lose form. You start thinking of defeat, and your defeatist thoughts create a cycle of underperformance that reinforces your defeatism. It is a vicious cycle. You talk yourself into losing. Break the cycle. Focus on one thing at a time. Winning the next point, positioning yourself in the right place – calling for the pass and focusing on your job, everything else is unnecessary. <u>Live in the present</u>. When SEALs are undertaking their training they are taught to think only as far as the current task or component of the task in hand: completing the endurance run, finishing the swim, making it through to lunch. Whether you are fighting for your life or for a gold medal, <u>focus on the here and now</u>.

Increase resilience with anchoring

If you notice that your game is going to pieces, that your blocks are too slow, and think you are going to lose, break the cycle. Breathe deeply, and use the anchors discussed in the previous chapter (page 86). Then cheer yourself on. Say encouraging things to yourself, and imagine yourself or your team winning. Then go back to focusing on the present.

Whenever you notice your attention is straying from the game or the fight, breathe deeply, reactivate the appropriate anchors and focus on the task at hand.

Furthermore, try rehearsing this process mentally, so that you go from feeling flustered or defeated, to relaxed, to encouraged, to focused. After each mental rehearsal let your mind go blank and think about something different so you aren't linking positive thoughts directly back to negative ones and creating a loop. By practising this mental thought process you can turn it into a habit so that when you are on the field or in the ring, you can apply it easily and quickly. This will help make you unflappable when you and your team are in tight corners.

Dealing with trauma

Another area which deeply affects resilience and performance is trauma. Trauma can take many forms and can be caused by numerous events. While this section talks about psychological trauma it is important to note that most injuries, especially serious injuries, affect you psychologically as well. There are many cases where athletes have lost their edge after sporting injuries or from instances of on-field bullying. Being able to recover from the psychological consequences of traumatic experiences is vital for athletes who want to continue performing at their best. Furthermore, the basic techniques taught here can be applied to a number of other situations increasing the effectiveness of other visualisations.

These techniques were first developed in the 1970s working with Vietnam veterans suffering from post traumatic stress disorder (PTSD).

Peter D. Campbell

Several applications of this process have been used after major disasters including the 1987 Lockerby bombing incident in Scotland. It has been successfully used with victims of the civil wars in the former Yugoslavia and Chechnya, as well as following the September 11 terrorist attacks, and also in the aftermath of earthquakes and tsunamis. While many psychologists claim there is still no way to treat PTSD, numerous cases show that the techniques explained below are effective. An increasing body of scientific evidence shows this method does effectively treat the condition.[24] I have successfully used these techniques with dozens of sportspeople and also victims of violent crime and earthquake survivors. It is therefore not only applicable to improving your sporting success, it can be applied to other areas of your life.

When discussing setting goals (page 33) we experimented a little with their visual representations. As a general principle we tend to imagine important items and events as being

---

[24] For a good discussion on the subject see Dr. Richard M. Gray, "NLP and PTSD: the Visual-Kinesthetic Dissociation Protocol", *Current Research in NLP: vol 2 - Proceedings of 2010 Conference*. At time of writing the article could be found at: http://www.anlp.org/files/nlp-and-ptsd-the-visual-kinesthetic-dissociation-protocol_6_331.pdf; View also http://www.researchandrecognition.org/#!about1/c206e.

The Champion

large and nearby. You will probably have noticed that movies are scarier or more dramatic when you see them at a movie theatre than when you see them on a small screen. When people suffer an injury or a serious setback they hold large images of these experiences close before for them – it is almost as if their subconscious never wants them to forget what a terrible experience it was. Consequently, such traumas can have a disproportionate influence on our lives.

When interviewing people who suffered PTSD and comparing their answers with people who had experienced similar events and suffered no trauma, it was discovered that traumatised people remembered the experiences from a first person perspective, whereas people who were not traumatised remember the experiences as if in the third person, and often as if the experiences were happening to someone else.

In order to reduce the influence of such experiences we can practice re-defining these large, hurtful images as smaller and innocuous images. This means that through repetition the mental association you have with the traumatic experience can be reduced and ultimately eliminated.

Peter D. Campbell

Overcoming traumatic experiences

The following mental rehearsal enables you to dramatically reduce psychological trauma. It may seem strangely metaphysical but the technique is designed to dissociate you from the events. Read over the exercise first so that you know what to expect and then do every stage of the exercise.

1. Imagine entering a movie theatre. The screen is small and is located a long way away.
2. You take a seat right at the back of the theatre.
3. On the distant screen you can see an image of yourself before the incident and an image of yourself after the incident when you have recovered.
4. Both images are in black and white.
5. Now imagine floating up out of your body and going into the projection room at the movie theatre. From here it will be possible to watch yourself watching a movie.
6. In the projection room you have complete control over everything, and shortly you will play a movie of the events that had traumatized you, viewing it from the first

The Champion

image of yourself to the second image of yourself.

7. Focus on the person sitting in front of you (yourself), so that you are watching someone watching a movie. This creates an additional step of distancing you from the events. While looking at the person in front of you, play the entire movie from the first image of yourself to the second image of yourself.

8. Once you have reached the end of the movie, go back down into your own body and then go all the way down to the screen and jump into the movie at the end.

9. Over 1.5 seconds, rewind at high speed the entire movie with you participating in the events. Trauma is an experience that moves forward, you were traumatized <u>after</u> the event. By rehearsing the incident backwards you are practising experiencing the incident in a way which <u>undoes</u> the trauma.

10. Let your mind go blank, think of something completely different. What you ate today, what you want to do on the weekend, when will you meet with friends etc. Think of any

random thing which is unrelated to what you are currently doing.

11. After a brief pause, repeat the exercise. About seven times should be sufficient to noticeably reduce the sense of anxiety you experience when thinking about the incident.

To do this process the first time usually takes quite a lot of time and concentration. As you become familiar with the process and as the trauma recedes, you will find it becomes easier and faster. After you have done the process a couple of times you can add background music to make the event seem even less important – try adding the theme song from some absurd comedy such as Monty-Python's Flying Circus, or imagine music from a 1920s silent movie.

If you are in a hurry and need to speed this process up, simply do the steps for rewinding the experience. MRI scans indicate that this step is sufficient to alter the neurology and can by itself reduce trauma.

When to use the trauma cure

The most obvious time to use this technique is after a particularly bad performance. I once coached a racing car driver who used to go to pieces after a crash and was unable to race aggressively for the rest of the day. Using this technique immediately after a crash he could get back immediately to racing aggressively. If you play a bad game, have a bad fight, feel depressed or despondent about your performance, use this technique. The ability to distance yourself from bad experiences dramatically increases your resilience.

Recovering from injuries

Sportspeople will often suffer from injuries and frequently these become recurring injuries. Even when you have recovered and strengthened the muscles involved there often seems to be a residual weakness which makes it easy to re-injure the muscle. Some injuries just seem to take a really long time to heal.

There are several elements to injuries. If you are taking a long time to recover from an injury or you are frequently being injured, it might be due to bad diet and can be resolved simply by increasing the amount of protein you are eating. There may be technical reasons for a recurrent injury: perhaps your technique is faulty, and that is causing injuries. While you continue to use it, you can expect to get injured. There might also be physiological reasons for injuries, your body might be the wrong shape for the activity you are trying to do, you might have a muscle imbalance, or your muscles, tendons, and ligaments mightn't be strong enough for the demands being made of them.

If you exclude all of these other reasons and you continue to experience injury, or an injury takes a long time to heal, there may be a psychological reason behind it.

The most obvious psychological causes for physical injury is self-sabotage (see section on Self-Sabotage, page 145), where for some reason something inside you seems to want you to fail. This might be because the sport is overly dangerous, or participation is distracting you from other, potentially more important activities; or perhaps you have such a history of failure that the expectation of failure has become reinforced; it might be the result of a previous trauma.

Injuries are often memorable – etching themselves into your memory as if engraved in stone. Because they are often dramatic, extremely painful, emotional and (fortunately) rare, they are extremely memorable. The problem with this though is that images and ideas which are subconsciously held in close proximity also act as instructions for how you should behave. It is as if the force of the traumatic experience is such that it re-programmes your 'control centre'. It is therefore likely that one reason why people re-injure is simply that they have the injury foremost of the subconscious. This would also explain why some injuries take substantially longer to heal than others. By using the above trauma cure for experiences that have injured you, you can shorten injury recovery times and reduce your susceptibility to future injury.

For several years I was unable to fence because of knee trouble. One afternoon I was pondering the connection between body and mind and out of curiosity tried the trauma cure on my knees. Something changed. That same afternoon I went to the beach and was able to bound from rock to rock, something I had been unable to do for years because I couldn't trust my knees to hold. Having taken up fencing again, I have never had a knee injury.

However, <u>these techniques do not save you from injury entirely</u>. Your muscles and their attachments still have to be strengthened and trained to perform what you are requiring of them! For example if I do a lot of walking and no fencing training, a muscle imbalance develops in my thighs, which leads to knee injuries when I fence.

I have used this technique with several athletes who have had ongoing injuries. All of them have noticed improvements although in a couple of cases the injury required substantial rehabilitation work to rebuild and strengthen the muscle.

Other visualisations for injury recovery

While the trauma cure is an excellent technique to recover from injury there are two other visualisations that I have found useful. One of these was my first introduction to neuro-linguistic programming and was so successful that it led me to start studying the subject and eventually train in it.

In December 2005, on a frosty evening I was walking home late from work, when a thug attacked me. In the ensuing fight I received a broken nose and third-degree concussion. After three days in hospital I was released and told to take things easy for a couple of weeks. While I quickly recovered from the initial injuries which were largely superficial, I suffered from ongoing and constant head-aches. After half a day at work a severe head-ache would come on, and my eyes would hurt. My right eye which had been pummelled several times would become unbearably painful. In the evening, after work I would come home and listen to audiobooks until eventually I fell asleep. This continued for week,

The Champion

after week, after week. After four months I was still in severe pain. I spoke to friends who had suffered concussions and many of them complained that even after several years, they still couldn't read for very long periods.

One evening I was talking to a friend of mine and he suggested the following visualisation. I was sceptical but I didn't have anything to lose; it wasn't as if I was stretched for time. He suggested the following:

1. Imagine that you are lying on your back, floating in a warm, pleasant river.
2. The water washes down to you nutrients and minerals that heal your body.
3. Lying there, with the water washing past and through you, bringing nutrients and minerals that heal you, it washes away all the injury, all the pain. It washes away the negative emotions and heals you, fully and completely.

I lay in bed and just imagined I was floating on my back in a river. As I lay there, watching my floating body, I could see what looked like black blood being washed away from my head. It continued bleeding for a long time. I fell asleep doing the exercise, but on waking felt better. Then lying there waiting to fall asleep again I thought about the nature of sleep and of dreams and thought that a visualisation is pretty much a dream and thought that perhaps I could just dream this visualisation all night long while I was sleeping. I fell asleep some time and woke up next morning.

It was a one night cure. When I awoke the pain was completely gone and it did not return. I am aware that many people who suffer a concussion are affected by it for months and even years. It can severely reduce working ability and quality of life. I am also aware that in some cases this exercise by itself is not sufficient to cure concussion, although it was in my case. However, I have used this visualisation with clients, some of whom have spent an entire week using it and have achieved remarkable improvements in their health. If you have an injury which is not responding to normal treatment, this visualisation is worth a try. I used a similar visualisation on another occasion when I was recovering from surgery and by all accounts had a very fast and full recovery.

The Champion

Unlearning bad habits and installing good ones

How do you unlearn bad habits? Usually we have to practice good habits until at some stage they override the bad habit. But what is a bad habit? It is a form of behaviour that recurs involuntarily. The trauma cure was originally designed for therapy to stop people from performing involuntary behaviour (flashbacks, anxiety, phobic reactions etc). As with trauma, bad habits are usually behaviour which is subconsciously held close to us and so while bad habits may not be traumatic, they can still be removed by using a visualisation technique to undo the reinforcement that the bad habits have had over the years, and replace them with a different pattern of behaviour.

To unlearn a habit

1. Imagine a small screen in front of you, about the size of a cell-phone screen 20-30 metres away from you.

2. See yourself performing the entire bad habit from start to finish in black and white.

3. Go into the experience and over 1.5 seconds experience doing the bad habit backwards.

4. Let your mind go blank and think about something completely different.

5. Repeat this exercise at least seven times.

To install a habit

See the section *Learning new skills* (page 71). If you are unfamiliar with the new habit, it is best to go through the entire process of learning it. If you already know how to perform the technique and can do it, but simply found that you tended to revert to the old habit, you can simply use visualisation to implant the new habit so that it fully supplants the old one. Try the following rehearsal:

1. Imagine seeing yourself performing the technique you want to develop.

2. See this as a large movie, close to you.

3. Make the images in the movie bright, clear and attractive

4. Having watched yourself performing the technique perfectly, step into the movie and play it again, with you participating in it. Imagine all of the sounds, the smells, the feelings that you would be experiencing when you perform this technique in real life.

5. Having completed the movie, let your mind go blank.

6. Repeat this exercise at least seven times.

As we tend to carry out actions that have been coded as being close to us (believing them to be more important), this technique replaces a bad habit with a good habit. The more often you practice the visualisation for installing a new habit, the better you will be at it – but to start with, try repeating it seven times and you will already notice improvements.

How I learnt to serve

In my childhood I used to play tennis and although I became quite good I never mastered a reliable serve. As I grew up I moved onto other sports and only played tennis occasionally with friends and family for fun.

Peter D. Campbell

I was playing a game with friends not long after I had become interested in sports psychology and being ashamed of my erratic serve decided then and there to learn to serve well. I had childhood memories of the occasional good serve that I placed in court, and which on rare occasions was devastating to my opponents.

To correct my serve, this is what I did:

1. I remembered a time when I served a fabulous ace. I remembered the experience in as much detail as I could, remember the court, the weather, who I was playing with, the feel of the sun, the feel of my muscles as I went through the entire serve.

2. Having recollected and visualised a time when I served the perfect serve, I then imagined that all of those sensations for the serve I was about to make, and watching how I would strike the ball and it would whizz into the court at high speed and thud into the netting behind the court, acing my opponent.

3. Serve.

Using this process I went from an erratic serve which would go into court only two or three times out of ten, to a serve that went into court eight or nine times out of ten. I didn't ace my opponents very often. But the serve was good, strong and reliable. You will notice that in step one, the visualisation of recollecting a time when I made a very good serve is the same as is used for establishing an anchor to get you into another state (such as a state of flow).

Now you might wonder how this helps if you have never experienced doing the technique really well. In that case, you should go through the full learning process described on page 71 as that process is designed to ensure that you learn a skill properly and thoroughly so that you can execute it perfectly every time.

Peter D. Campbell

Increasing speed

In most sports speed is a vital element, whether you need to block and attack quickly in martial arts, move a ball quickly around your opponents in soccer or hockey, or being able to respond to a ball hit or thrown at you.

There are several elements to speed which authors break down into various parts. A simple break down is as follows:

- Perception time: you cannot respond if you cannot perceive;
- Response time: the time it takes to make a decision about how to handle a situation and then to respond to it,
- Speed of movement: the time it takes to move.[25]

---

[25] As defined by Loren W. Christensen in *Speed Training: How To Develop Your Maximum Speed For Martial Arts*. Different writers break the elements of speed into different categories, Bruce Lee in

The Champion

Each sport has its own drills for developing speed but there are three principles that athletes need to follow to increase speed:

Muscle: fast-twitch muscle is faster than slow-twitch muscle. How fast you are depends on what type of muscle you have, and this depends on genetics, and on the sort of training you do. Relaxed muscle is faster than taut muscle.

1. Practice: an important element for increasing speed is practice, lots of practice..
2. Perception of time: As Einstein said "time is relative", but little did he know how relative it is. Like beauty, it is in the eye of the beholder and there are psychological techniques that can be used to accelerate perception.

Muscle type

Fast twitch muscle fibre is necessary for fast movements. This is the sort of muscle that is developed when you do exercises of up to ten repetitions. Contrary to popular belief big

---

The Tao of Jeet Kune Do, for example, breaks speed into five categories: perceptual speed, mental speed, initiation speed, performance speed and alteration speed. Regardless of how they are categorized they cover the same skills and processes.

muscles do not necessarily mean slow muscles – they are slow if you focus on hypertrophic exercises (10-14 repetitions). Often when you need speed you want to have explosive speed – you can help train your muscles for this by doing plyometric exercises. These are exercises where you jump, pump, punch with fast, quick movements.

Another obstacle that can slow athletes down is tension. If your muscles are straining with a weight – if a racket, club, bat, epée etc is too heavy for you, you will have to strain to use it and this will slow you down dramatically. The fundamental element to being fast is having the <u>strength</u> to move quickly.

Tension created by stress, bullying, anxiety and fear will also affect your speed and in such cases you should apply an anchor to relax you (refer to page 86). If you have an ongoing problem with tension and stress you need to find the cause and then deal with it. The trauma cure discussed above (page 102) is a good way of resolving fears and anxieties, as is hypnosis (refer to page 157.

The Champion

Practice

There is nothing like practice to make you good at something and fast at something. Loren W Christensen, author of *Speed Training: How to Develop Your Maximum Speed for Martial Arts*, notes that Bob Munden, who refers to himself as "the fastest gun the West has ever known" used to do 3500 draws every four days when he was training, whereas his rival do only about 200. Practice doing a technique slowly, make sure all elements are correct and then practice it repeatedly increasing the speed while maintaining good technique.

Speed training techniques vary from sport to sport. For martial arts striking at a moving target, or a retreating target is good speed training. In sports such as tennis, cricket, baseball striking at ever faster balls helps to shorten response time.

Perception of time

Our perception of time differs depending on circumstances. When dreaming we can experience a complex series of events which seem to take minutes, hours or days within just a few seconds. When we are bored time seems to slow down, when we are interested it flies, and by altering our perception of time, we can change our reaction speeds when competing in sport. [26]

Ordinarily when driving a car around town, 50 or 60 km/h seems to be a normal speed, not too slow, not overly fast. However, if you have been driving at 100 km/h on the open road, slowing down to 60 km/h seems unbearably slow. Your perception of time has adjusted to the higher speed.

How it is that professional tennis players can have time to respond to and return a ball which is served at 230 km/h (130 mph) from only 24 metres away? Cricket batsmen react to a ball bowled at 140 km/h from only 20 metres away. One of the common lines of praise that sports commentators have for good batsmen is "it looks as though he has all the time in the world". A baseball pitcher pitches a ball at about 140 km/h (90 mph) 18 metres from the striker (60 feet). The fact that people can respond to these speeds

---

[26] David Eagleman carried out research into this effect which is known as the Oddball effect or as slow motion perception. Eagleman's conclusions was not that our perception of time had changed but that our recall of the event makes it appear to be stretched out. Research carried out using hypnosis by Dr. Milton Erickson and later by Dr. Richard Bandler would indicate that our perception of time does change – not simply the recall, however, conclusive scientific evidence is still lacking.

is remarkable. If you can alter your perception of speed it makes it possible to respond.

Traditionally, the only way to really alter your perception of speed is through lots of practice (see above) and indeed Dr. Richard Bandler, one of the co-founders of neuro-linguistic programming, has suggested that one of the main things that practice does is alter your perception of speed. However, by experimenting with visualisation Bandler and others have found ways to alter speed perception without the hours of training. Both Dr. Bandler and motivational guru Anthony Robbins have used these techniques with professional sportspeople to improve their performance.

While some people like to use anchoring or hypnosis to alter time perception the technique that I have found simplest and most effective is a simple visualisation called 'time distortion' which you rehearse as often as you can.

Time distortion

1. See yourself in the third person (dissociated) performing your sport.
2. Make this movie as real as possible in terms of setting, size, and colours. Make the image large and close to you.

3. Notice how quickly you move and respond in comparison to your opponent.

4. After watching your performance for a while, let the image of you approach you and step into your body.

5. As he steps into your body, he brings with him all of the knowledge and skills he has and possesses, including the fast reactions, reflexes and ability to perform at a high level, really quickly.

6. Let this knowledge spread throughout your body, through every muscle, carried through your blood to every cell and molecule.

7. Now visualise performing your sport again, but this time you are doing it from a first person point of view (associated). Your actions appear, look and feel to you to be occurring at a normal speed, but the actions of your opponents seem to be extremely slow, giving you time to respond to the situation easily.

8. Having spent some time enjoying this visualisation, let your mind go blank. Think about something else for a while. Repeat the entire process several times.

The Champion

This is one of the most effective and useful visualisations you will ever encounter. It is so effective that I almost did not include it in this book as it would be disadvantageous to me to have my sporting competitors know my secrets; however, leading NLP practitioners are aware of it and so I might as well get some of the credit for advertising it.

A slightly different approach to this technique is suggested by Loren W. Christensen in his book *Speed Training: How To Develop Your Maximum Speed For Martial Arts.* He recommends a visualisation procedure for copying technique and speed from other people, which he calls 'head-swapping.' This is a process where you imagine someone who performs a technique quickly or well – and then you "swap heads", meaning that you perceive yourself carrying out the actions like someone else. Christensen has spent 40-odd years doing martial arts and serving on the streets as a policeman. He claims that this technique is beneficial, however there are several variations that could make it more effective. I recommend that you experiment and find what works best for you.

Peter D. Campbell

Techniques for learning from others and increasing speed

1. Choose someone who you want as a role model for your sport.

2. Watch that person performing, demonstrating all of the skills and abilities you want to acquire (technical skill, speed, etc).

3. Then see that sportsperson come off the field/ring/do-jo/piste and approach you.

4. Here you have two options, either the sportsperson gives a special gift or a talisman which embodies his/her skills, or you can let your image of the sportsperson become a part of you, guiding you in your sport.

5. When you receive the gift/sportsperson, receive it and let it become a part of you. Imagine the person stepping into your body and bringing with him, all of the skills and qualities that make that person good at sport, or if receiving a gift imagine accepting the gift and the gift becoming a part of you.

6. As you imagine step 5, feel how the skills and abilities that are being given/brought

The Champion

to you by the sportsperson spread throughout your body, through your blood, through your brain, through your muscles, your limbs, through every cell and molecule of your body.

7. Having fully and completely accepted these skills and learnt from them, imagine yourself from a first person perspective (associated/point of view) performing the sport like your role model sportsperson.

Another variation on this theme is instead of visualising another sportsperson who you then model, is to imagine watching your future self who has already mastered the sport (linking in with the visualisation which was done as part of the goal setting and planning stage). You then watch how that future image of yourself performs perfectly, and then bring his/her skills and abilities into your current self. Each variation has its advantages and disadvantages. The swapping head technique is not as thorough as these other approaches but might be easier to do for some people. Other people might find the concept of bringing someone else into them off-putting while others might find it easier to model someone else, than modelling a future self. While all of these techniques work, they are dependent on your knowledge of how someone else performs, or how an ideal sportsperson performs in sport. This might require some research, you might like to watch numerous sporting videos of world class performers before trying this technique so that you know what your performance needs to become.

The Champion

Beliefs

Beliefs play a vital role in our lives. They determine what we want to do, they determine how much we enjoy what we do, and they determine the effort and the perseverance we are prepared to put into something to succeed.

For example someone who believes that "If it takes more than five minutes to learn, it's not worth learning," is unlikely to accomplish much in life. People who believe something is very hard often won't put in the effort to master it, as they have a belief that the effort required is greater than any possible reward. Some people, on the other hand, have beliefs that things are "too easy" and that the challenge is not great enough. For example, I am unlikely to ever take up dancing because my experience of it has led me to believe (wrongly) that it is too easy and I really don't understand why I should waste time learning to dance when I could spend it more enjoyably learning some other activity. However, such beliefs are more for guidance to help us make choices and lead a fulfilling life than an objective depiction of reality. I have no doubt that to become a world-class dancer requires just as much precision, determination, training – and in many cases strength – as to become a world class athlete.

An important example of the power of belief is the breaking of the four minute mile. On 6 May 1954 Roger Bannister broke a record that was thought impossible – running a mile in less than four minutes (3:59.8). The impossible had been proven to be possible after all, and his record stood for only 46 days. Since then over a thousand people have officially run four minute miles and even high school students have achieved it. The four minute mile was a psychological barrier – a matter of belief – and once that belief was discarded, the impossible became possible.

Your beliefs are not reality – they are your representation of reality and are only a guide to help you make decisions. Sometimes a belief or a series of beliefs hinder you and prevent you from achieving what you want. If you believe that "you always crack under pressure", that "you're not as talented as other people", that "you don't have time to train properly", that "you don't have the money to do well", "you are hopeless, you are weak, etc.", you will find that you constantly come up against obstacles. Such beliefs dis-empower you, neutralise your abilities, and will constrain ongoing training and competition performance. If you have beliefs such as: "When the going gets tough, the tough get going", "the bigger they are, the harder they fall", "there is always a way", "pain is weakness leaving the body", etc., then your performance resilience will be much higher. People usually only succeed if they believe that success is possible. If you want to succeed in sport, you need to make sure that your beliefs support what you want to achieve.

What do you believe in?

Our beliefs are often shown through how we behave and the things we say to ourselves and to others. Generalised statements often reveal beliefs that we hold. Think back to various challenges in your life. How do you behave in a crisis? How do you feel about accepting challenges? Do you feel excited and confident, uncertain, or defeated? Do you believe you can pull through by yourself? Do you think of yourself as 'focused'? Do you think of yourself as patient? Are you a 'go–getter'? Do you follow through and complete your projects? Do you achieve everything you put your mind to? Are you are winner?

Ask yourself these questions, and <u>really</u> ask yourself? Often we try to deceive ourselves: no one likes to admit to being a failure, even privately. Often when people complain that something is too easy, what they mean is that it is not sufficiently interesting – and sometimes that it is even too hard.

Write down the answers to these questions. This should give you some idea as to the beliefs you have.

Now try completing the following statements

I am the sort of person who….

I am naturally good at ….

When something bad happens I tend to ….

At the beginning of a competition I feel….

When I am about to compete against someone better than me I….

I am held back in my sport by….

I am good at my sport because….

The Champion

Answer as true or false:

I am more talented than others in my sport

I need to train more than others in my sport

I enjoy my sport more than others

I am good at my sport

I know I will get better

I get frustrated when things go wrong

I am generally a fast learner

Whenever I start to do well I self-sabotage

Whenever I start to do well I get injured or sick

I enjoy challenges

I lack patience

I am a winner

I can become a champion

I can make it to the national team

I want to be a champion

I am confident in my abilities as a sportsperson

When I train I give it everything I've got

When I compete I give it everything I've got

These questions should give you a good idea as to what beliefs guide you when training and competing. Make a list of your negative and positive beliefs.

Once you know what beliefs you have you can start changing the negative beliefs into positive beliefs. Some of these beliefs will be based on the results of previous performances. If this is the case, use the trauma cure explained on page 102 to distance yourself from those experiences. This will make you more amenable to changing the belief to a positive belief.

Remember that just because something happened to you once does not mean that it will always happen that way. Past performance, despite what HR managers might claim, does not determine future performance. Use the experience to perform and move on so that you do better next time. Every bad experience you have teaches you how to do something better (these are also useful beliefs to have – they will help keep you motivated and also help you continue to improve.

Changing beliefs

Once you know what beliefs you have, you can decide what beliefs you want to change. There are several ways to change beliefs, some are better than others. A common technique is simply to recite over and over verbal affirmations rather

The Champion

like Émile Coué's "Every day in every way I am getting better and better and better". In this case you would repeat over and over again the belief you want to have, e.g. "I am determined and successful". If you say this often enough, you will start to believe it, but there is a more elegant solution using principles that you have already learnt.

You know now that the visual imagery and proximity of that imagery influences how you relate to the reality. The same principle works for beliefs. The closer you hold the belief to you, the more it affects your subconscious behaviour.

Unhelpful beliefs are often easy to overcome. Once the subconscious recognises behaviour or ideas as being unhelpful, it often seems to deal with them automatically, but to help it along you can use the following technique:

1. Think of the belief you want to remove, for example "I always crack under pressure".

2. Now think of the opposite, positive belief that you would like to have instead of the old negative belief. If your belief was "I always crack under pressure", this might be changed to "I stay focused and perform best when under pressure".

3. As you think about the negative belief let an image that represents that belief come to mind. Often this image will be an occasion that justifies the belief, such as when you <u>did</u> crack under pressure.

4. As you see that image of the belief let it start to fade, become less distinct. Let the image start to shrink and move slowly away from you.

5. Let that image disappear into the distance and as it disappears let it be engulfed by a ball of flame so it is destroyed completely.

6. As the negative belief disappears over the horizon, let the image of the positive belief, starting out small, come flying towards you, as it gets closer it becomes bigger and bigger, more colourful and more real.

7. Bring the positive belief close to you so it sits in a space similar to what the old negative belief had.

8. Let your mind go blank. Think of something completely different for a few seconds then repeat the exercise so that you do it a total of seven times.

This is a very effective technique for removing old beliefs and installing new ones. I will often record the process onto a dictaphone (your home

The Champion

computer nowadays will have everything you need to record such exercises).[27] This is easy to do and then you can simply sit back and listen to the instructions and let the mind rearrange your beliefs. This is incredibly simple and powerful. The additional advantage of recording changes in belief is that if any old beliefs should return – for example after a bad performance, or bullying from other players or coaches, you can simply alter the belief by running the recording. If the belief is really an issue, people will often go into a trance while listening to the recording and will wake up at the end of the recording feeling a little disorientated.

Beliefs you should have

Here is a list of beliefs that are beneficial for sportspeople to have. It is designed primarily for those who want to be champions. The less serious sports person who simply wants to improve performance might leave off beliefs such as "I will do what it takes to win" and a certain amount of judgment should be used. If you do decide to do <u>everything</u> you can to win, you will perform more

---

[27] If you have any difficulty with the software that comes with your computer, download 'Audacity' and 'Lame for Audacity.' Both pieces of software are free and enable you to record and edit recordings. You can even insert music into a recording to make it more relaxing.

competitively but you might receive more injuries, the sport may also start to interfere with other activities and your relationships.

- I am talented at my sport
- I enjoy my sport
- I like winning
- I will become the best in my sport
- I improve constantly
- I perform well under stress
- I enjoy challenges
- I am a winner
- I will do what it takes to win (ethically)
- I stay calm and focused
- Pain is weakness leaving my body
- I learn quickly
- My body is strong and recovers quickly
- I am tactical and strategic
- I am fast and I am getting faster

If you think about these affirmative statements, and about your chosen sport, you will probably come up with some other beliefs that will be useful for you in sport (and in life) which you

The Champion

might like to add to this list. The reason why making these belief changes is useful and important is threefold. These beliefs:

1. help to motivate you;
2. increase the speed with which you learn (which also improves motivation and performance);
3. improve competition performance.

Peter D. Campbell

Performance personality and masks

When competing, sportspeople will often take on a performance personality. I have heard some sportspeople talk about the need to find their "sporting personality". You might have heard someone say, 'He's a different person when he is out there,' meaning that qualities of determination, aggression or concentration that are not usually evident, are on display. For some people this sporting personality is cheeky, for others it is cool and suave, while others still may find that it is simply bold and brutal. The type of personality, which is appropriate to you, depends on both the sport and your role. If you are uncertain, look at high performing sportspeople from your sport, whose style is similar to yours and analyse what personality they have when they are competing. Decide what elements of their performance personality you want to adopt.

Masks

Many nations and tribes around the world use masks as part of ceremonies, rites of passage and magic rituals. They are almost always used in a process of guiding an individual into a different state or status with different rules of behaviour. In the west we have similar behaviour but will often use costumes or clothes to represent these changes and play this role. It is similar to association and classical conditioning. On graduation, graduands wear different clothes from when they were students, and when they become employed wear different clothes again – representing different roles in society.[28] Soldiers will wear different clothes on the parade ground from that worn at a mess dinner or on the battlefield. Traditionally, when people attended festivals or parties they dressed differently. The popularity of fancy dress parties perhaps reflects this desire to change the environment and behaviour associated with it. A mask is therefore a way of stepping out of yourself and adopting a different set of personality traits for a limited period and is a useful technique for sportspeople

---

[28] These principles are now changing as life stages in western society become more undefined and unclear, and consequently more confusing.

and anyone who finds it necessary to perform in a certain way in specific circumstances. While some people create real masks, you can achieve a similar result by visualising the process.

1. Write down the main characteristics or traits you want to have while performing your sport. (If you are in a high profile sport, you might also want to create a media mask for dealing with press conferences or journalists). For sport these might include patience, calmness, control, masterfulness, finesse, energy, aggression, confidence, ferocity, slyness, cunning, ... depending on your sport and what your normal personality seems to lack.

2. Imagine standing on the side-lines, preparing to go onto the field (enter the ring etc.) and imagine that you hold in your hands your sporting mask.

3. As you hold the mask in your hands you see each of the skills and personality traits you want to have when you are competing falling into your mask. Some people see this as words, others see these traits as actual representations of the trait in use – so if it is patience they see themselves being patient in a sporting setting, if it is

The Champion

aggression, they see themselves being aggressive.

4. Once all the personality traits have entered the mask, imagine placing it on your face, and even carry out the action, placing the imaginary mask on your face.

5. As the mask fits onto your face, visualise all the personality traits being carried through your body, through every muscle and cell in your entire body.

6. Now view yourself performing in both a third person and first person (point of view), performing with this new performance personality.

Having carried out this exercise in the privacy of your home, whenever you are about to compete, take a moment to imagine placing the mask over your face.

Peter D. Campbell

Self-sabotage

One of the main complaints athletes make is about self-sabotage: "I had the game in the palm of my hand and I threw it away". There can be several causes for self-sabotage. Often it is the result of changing expectations and emotions about their success in a competition – in which fear of winning or losing often play a big part. The sections on *Anchoring* (page 86) and *Visualisation* (page 78) can be very helpful in limiting this form of self-sabotage.

Another common complaint which athletes call self-sabotage is injury. "Just as I am starting to perform well, I get injured" or "Just as I am getting fit enough to do well against the major players I get injured." In cases of injury it is worth reviewing my comments on fitness training (pages 44-66), ensuring that you have a diet which supports your body and the training you are doing, and make sure you work through the

The Champion

various elements associated with trauma (pages 105-116) and trying such techniques as the trauma cure.

Another common cause for self-sabotage is our beliefs surrounding self-identity, self-worth and self-confidence. Such beliefs can cause people to freeze up, lose focus, or even quit a sport for seemingly no real reason. Such beliefs can also lead to injury as the subconscious seeks ways and justifications for not performing (see section on *Beliefs* pages 130-140).

While all of these approaches and techniques are useful and in some cases critical when dealing with cases of self-sabotage, often athletes simply complain that "it is almost like a part of me is holding me back". Common beliefs which lead to self-sabotage often relate to finding a balance between sport and other commitments and are sometimes best dealt with by negotiating with the part. The technique you are about to learn enables you to negotiate with such parts.

The problem is that often in life we are drawn in different directions by conflicting hopes, goals, duties and desires. How often can someone in true honesty say that they really want something fully and completely without reservation? Often we do have reservations, we want to succeed but we don't want it to affect our friendships, or our career, or what people think of us. We all have our own demons and ghosts which at some stage seem to hold us up or hold us back. If you notice yourself saying something similar to "It's almost as if there is a part of me which doesn't want me to succeed/do this," or if you have a feeling that you are not 100% committed to your goal, then the following exercise is often a quick and elegant way of resolving the problem. The technique enables you to discuss and persuade whatever it is within you that is causing the self-sabotage. The exercise seems bizarre but is often effective and can be done quite quickly. If this exercise doesn't solve the self-sabotage, then it is simply a matter of working your way through the other visualisation techniques until the negative behaviour disappears. This current technique is referred to as Parts Integration and enables us to negotiate with a subconscious part that is generating the self-sabotaging behaviour. The technique makes the assumption that this part is attempting to look after your best interests, and that the self-sabotage is an effort to help you. This is done in the following manner:

The Champion

Parts integration

1. Place your hands in front of you and ask the part generating the self-sabotaging behaviour to come out of you and sit/stand in your left hand. Ask yourself what does it look like? How does it feel? What temperature is it? Does it move? What size is it? People give a variety of answers, sometimes the part is large and heavy, sometimes small, sometimes it looks like them, often it looks like an unhappy version of themselves. In general there is a wide variety, so work with whatever options come to mind. Often people don't actually "see" or "feel" the part but answers just come to mind. Work with these. Once the part has come out, thank it for appearing and being prepared to "talk" with you.

2. Ask the part of you which wants to achieve your sporting goal and ask it to come out of you and sit/stand in your right hand. Ask yourself the same questions what does it look like? How does it feel? What temperature is it? Does it move? What size is it? The image which often appears for athletes is of them wearing a medal, or on a podium. Sometimes it is a cup

representing victory. Representations vary from individual to individual. Once the part has come out, thank it for appearing and being prepared to "talk" with you.

3. Still focusing on that part in your right hand, tell it that you understand that it wants to help you. Ask it what its intention is. What does it want? Wait until some answer appears in your mind. Often it will appear to be extremely simple and prosaic.

4. Once you have the answer, ask it to imagine that it has that intention completely and fully, and having that intention completely and fully, ask it what it wants which is even more important. Wait until an answer comes to mind.

5. Continue asking this question. As you receive answers and reiterate the question you will find yourself going through a list of wants and desires that represent the sort of person you are. Often when people finally reach the end of the iteration, they find that what they really want is happiness, peace, love, or a sense of oneness or wholeness. Once you have reached the final iteration ...

The Champion

6. Turn your attention back to the part in your left hand, and tell it that you understand that it wants to help you. Ask it what it is trying to achieve through the behaviour (which you perceive as self-sabotage), ask it what its intention is. Wait until some answer appears in your mind. Often it will appear to be simple and prosaic.

7. Once you have the answer, ask it to imagine that it has that intention completely and fully, and having that intention completely and fully, ask it what it wants which is even more important. Wait until an answer comes to mind.

8. Continue asking this question until you start getting the same answers as you received for your right hand. This demonstrates to both parts that they have the same goals and aims and are simply working against each other to try to achieve them. Ask the part in the left hand if it recognizes this? Usually, it will. Sometimes it won't, in which case you need to continue following the intentions further until you reach the identical highest intention (peace, calm, etc).

9. When the two parts have agreed that they share the same intentions ask them if they can now work together to achieve the same goals. Often, at this point the left hand will be reluctant because it has very good reasons (as it perceives them) for generating self-sabotaging behaviour. You can then ask it what it needs in order to cooperate with your right hand. This is where you need to start negotiations and often your right hand will need to agree to some of the needs of the left hand.

10. Conduct the negotiations between the hand asking each what it wants and what it needs. They usually come to an agreement quite quickly.

11. Having agreed the two parts can then recognize that they can work together to achieve your sporting goals and you can then place your hands together. When they do come together people often see the parts merging and becoming a single representation. You can then let this united, single part, return to your body. Some people visualize this process, others "place" it inside themselves by bringing their hands to their stomach, or to their heart.

The Champion

This process can be done quite quickly, although in some case it can take a long time. Furthermore, on completing it people will often feel "spaced out" and "not themselves" for a while. What you have done is resolve conflicting emotions by objectifying them. It is actually quite a draining process because you have gone deeply into your psyche. If you need to drive somewhere following this technique, go for a brisk walk to clear your head and recover before driving.

Peter D. Campbell

Self talk

As discussed in the chapter on resilience (page 96), how you talk to yourself plays an important role in how resilient you are, how motivated you are and ultimately how successful you become. That voice in your head is a full time training coach to give you pep talks whenever you need it. It can also be your worst critic and enemy, lying to you and saying things that you don't need to hear, and distracting you from what you need to do. To master yourself, master the voices in your head.

If you watch people practice by themselves, pay attention to the language they use when they start making errors. Often they will make broad generalisations based on one error. Someone who makes a double-fault in tennis will start telling themselves that they "can't serve". The "I can't" mind-frame is endemic and is often imported into sport from life in general. These

The Champion

statements become suggestions/instructions for how you perform and impede improvement. One of the key problems with negative self talk is it tends to be generalised. We don't say "today at 3.15 I made a bad serve", we generalise it to say "I can't serve" meaning that we never have and never will be able to serve.

There are several ways of dealing with negative self talk. The easiest and most obvious way is to talk back. Every time you notice yourself making a negative statement is to challenge the statement. Ask yourself the following questions:

- When specifically can't I? How often can I?
- According to whom? Who says I can't? What did they actually mean? Is there any reason to think that what they said on one occasion has any significance for me as a sportsperson in general?

By repeatedly challenging negative self-talk, asking for specific details and examples, you will begin to recognise that negative self-talk is largely wrong. For people who have had the idea that "they'll never amount to anything" drummed into them this can be challenged with questions like: "when exactly don't I amount to anything?", "how often do I amount to something?", "who says I won't amount to anything?", "what exactly is anything?", "what did he/she actually mean by 'amount' and 'anything'?". By demanding specific examples you demonstrate that negative self talk is generalising unusual behaviour, rather than reflecting usual behaviour.

Another way to approach negative self talk is by doing a technique similar to the parts integration used for working with self sabotage (page 145).

Changing the voice in your head

1. Listen to the voice. Pay attention to what it is saying, notice the tone, the volume and the rhythm. Identify who is the voice in your head. Often these voices come from adults in our youth and are phrases, which we were frequently told. They can often also be voices which we heard when we were impressionable (for example going through difficult times in our lives, or under significant stress), coaches' and drill sergeants' voices often get imprinted as a result of this stress.

2. After identifying whose voice is talking to you, see them, observe their face and body language as they speak to you.

3. Expand the scope of what you can see to the context behind the events. Understand the reasons why they are talking to you the

The Champion

way they are. What does this reveal about them? How does it change the meaning of what they were telling you?

4. Now imagine that you are talking to that person today and ask them what they really meant to say and what they wanted to do? What was their real intention? Thank them for trying to help.

5. Identify a trusted friend who cares for you and who encourages you the way you want to be encouraged. If you are unable to think of someone whose voice you would like to use, you can use either your own, or decide what sort of voice you would like to hear to encourage you.

6. Change voices. Ask the original person's voice, whether it would be prepared to use this other voice, which you will listen to attentively, it can always return to the old voice if the new one doesn't work.

Peter D. Campbell

Hypnosis and sport

Hypnosis is another effective technique for working with your subconscious. It works by placing you in a relaxed state of mind and closes down parts of the brain associated with critical thinking. This enables you to make suggestions to your subconscious to behave in certain ways, or do certain things. Hypnosis is largely the state of being suggestible and suggestion is powerful. A good example of this power is the placebo effect.

The placebo effect occurs when a doctor gives you medication for a condition. You take the medication and your condition improves and sometimes is even cured. However, the medication was no more than a sugar pill. The placebo is simply a suggestion to your body to recover, and gives you permission to do so. It is so dramatic that pharmaceutical companies have to be careful to do blind tests on patients to discover whether a new drug is effective or whether it is simply a placebo. Interestingly enough, if the doctor believes that the placebo being prescribed is real prescription medicine, the placebo is more effective. Similarly, the more impressive the placebo appears, the greater the likelihood of it being effective. For example, a high tech piece of machinery is more effective than an injection, a syringe is more effective than a capsule, a capsule more effective than a pill. The bigger the item, the flashier the packaging, the greater the chances that the placebo is effective.

Hypnosis places people in a state where they can accept a range of suggestions which then are accepted and acted upon by the subconscious. An athlete can use hypnosis to recover more quickly from injury, or even use it as an anaesthetic, but more importantly, it can be used to improve performance.

Have you ever attended a hypnotist show and watched one of the standard tricks where a subject is invited onto the stage, is hypnotised, and after being given suggestions to be incredibly strong, is able to lie across two chairs in a plank, their body rigid. This is an impressive act, but it is even more impressive when the hypnotist gets someone to then stand on the belly of the person doing the bridge and the bridge does not collapse.

Peter D. Campbell

Psychological studies show that people only use between 30 and 50 percent of their actual muscle strength. Once we reach that load, the central nervous system kicks in and gives instructions not to lift anymore to avoid injury. In times of crisis or extreme danger, increased levels of cortisone and adrenalin clamp down on these natural limitations imposed by the central nervous system and enable people to achieve seemingly super-human feats. This is why in emergencies people are capable of lifting cars off accident victims and how people in earthquakes are suddenly able to lift and hurl away concrete blocks to free people trapped under rubble. However, you don't need to be in an emergency to achieve these feats: there are two ways of being able to achieve this super-human strength. One is through deliberately training with heavy weights to train your central nervous system, which is what weight lifters do. They often reach 80 percent of total lifting capacity and in competition can even reach 90 percent total capacity. The other technique is to use hypnosis. A combination of the two works wonders.

However, hypnosis can be used not just for increasing strength. Hypnosis is a process, which enables you to talk directly with your subconscious. For this reason you can use hypnosis to achieve most of the results we have previously discussed using visualisation techniques. You can use hypnosis to reduce anxiety, respond to performance fears, to bring you into a state of flow for a competition, to alter perception of time. Furthermore, people who have difficulty doing specific visualisation techniques can be hypnotised and can then do visualisations under hypnosis. When working with clients I prefer to use this technique. Instead of just giving clients a suggestion to feel motivated about training, I will also specifically walk them through a process which I know will make them motivated to train– although usually a suggestion is sufficient.

Everyone goes into trance – Everyone can be hypnotised

Many people claim that hypnosis does not work, or that it won't work with them because they can't be hypnotised. Others fear that they will be made to do things they don't want to do when hypnotised. These impressions are largely the result of stage hypnosis where people do outrageous things. When people attend these shows and fail to be hypnotized or see people doing weird things, it can leave them with incorrect impressions about hypnosis.

Peter D. Campbell

Hypnosis is a state of relaxed focus. There are varying levels of hypnosis, sometimes people are simply in a light trance, other times they seem to go into a state which is almost indistinguishable from sleep. However, the state is one of relaxation and attention. Everyone naturally goes into these states – and usually does so frequently throughout the day. If you watch television or a movie and become so involved with what is portrayed that you become unaware of your surroundings, you have entered a state of trance (trance is the same as hypnosis). When you drove home from work and had no recollection of the trip when you arrived, you were in a state of trance. Do you 'zone out' from time to time in the course of the day, just staring out of the window, or at a dot on the wall, or into blank space? That is another case of trance. When using self-hypnosis the aim is simply to focus on yourself and relax, and then enter a meditative state – you start making suggestions. As you can see, anyone is capable of doing this.

However, not everyone is prepared to let someone else guide them through the process. This is where the myth of hypnotizable and non-hypnotizable people developed. People who seem to be difficult to hypnotise are usually just reluctant to let other people do it to them. In the appropriate environment, they can be as easily hypnotised as anyone else. Although it is best to go to a competent hypnotist to deal with complicated issues, self-hypnosis is possible and effective, and will save you money.

Self-hypnosis inductions

Self-hypnosis is easily done and can be highly effective. There are numerous hypnotic inductions to go into trance, but the basic principle for all of them remains the same: Focus on something, relax and maintain the focus. Typically, people will either close their eyes and focus on their breathing. They then imagine walking down a staircase into a lovely place – I often use a staircase cut into rocky cliffs leading down to a deserted, Mediterranean beach. Counting from ten to one as you take each step. When you reach one, you will be in a light trance and able give yourself suggestions. The problem of using this method of self-hypnosis is that you have to maintain sufficient awareness to give yourself suggestions and maintain awareness of the process. A good way to improve the effectiveness of self-hypnosis is to record an induction, include the suggestions and then listen to it. This has the advantage that you can listen to the hypnosis again if necessary. Stephen Gilligan, one of the world's leading clinical hypnotherapists, suggests that clients should listen to his recordings for three weeks for the new habit to become entrenched. In my own work with clients and using self-hypnosis I have found that this is often unnecessary. However, humans are highly susceptible to their environment, events and emotional states. Any one of these can be sufficient to undo suggestions offered under hypnosis – so it is often useful to replay hypnotic recordings, or sometimes update them for a new change in circumstances. This is not to say the Stephen Gilligan is wrong; there have been cases where I have had to use hypnotic recordings over and over again to be certain of the benefits, but often this is not required or necessary. Experiment to see what works for you.

Hypnotic induction

The following is a hypnotic induction that I often use and is very successful. Instead of trying to relax you first, it invites you to remember a time when you were relaxed and to step into the experience. It then takes you from that relaxed state into a state of focused relaxation by turning your attention inwards. This will carry you into a trance where you can then offer suggestions. Some people will go into a deep trance – others will just be in light state of trance and might feel that the recording has failed. It hasn't, even light

The Champion

trances can be powerful, usually a light trance is all that is necessary for people to improve their sport or to stop smoking.

Record the following induction[29], read slowly and when you see three dots, that means you can leave a pause. This gives the mind time to respond to the instruction.

Lie back and relax and think of a time when you were really truly relaxed ... a time when you were on the point of sleep ... you know that feeling at the end of a long, tiring day when you lie down, tired, and think that you might just do something for a little while before going to sleep ... but your eyes close and almost instantly you fall away into a deep, deep sleep ... and just imagine doing that now, when I say relax ... and when I say relax, that means that you can relax totally ... fully taking the time to enjoy how the muscles in your neck and body start to lengthen... that's right, you can begin to feel that relaxation and as you notice how your muscles in your neck and shoulders relax you might notice that warmth spreading throughout your body ... and you might be wondering, after all

---

[29] Most mobile phones have a recording function, as do computers. To edit audio files you can download Audacity and Lame for Audacity free, which give you the capacity to edit, mix and save as mp3 files any recordings you make.

its good to wonder ... and you might wonder just how relaxed you can become, now .... that's right, and take a deep breath in and turn your attention inwards ... as you really begin to enjoy the depth of your relaxation you can focus on the sound of my voice and that means you are falling deeper .... into another state, a deeper state where your mind can make changes ... and you don't mind, do you? After all, it is your mind ... And you may not even have noticed yet, how your breathing is slowing down ... just as you are slowing down inside ... That's right, and that means that you are going even deeper into trance, now. And as you go deeper into a state of trance, your conscious mind might like to wonder ... wonder what it was that I was saying four sentences ago ... and as you realise with amusement how hard it is to remember ... what it was that I said four or five sentences ago ... you might be surprised at how deeply you are in trance already ...

That's right ... and as you wonder you may notice how slowly you are breathing ... which means that you are going even deeper into trance ... that's right ... and as you notice just how slowly you are breathing ... you might also notice that the sounds are becoming slower ... and that means that you are already in a deep ... deep trance... and you can continue to take that trance deeper still ... to a

The Champion

place deep inside where you are completely still ... that's right ... now ... you can find yourself in a place where change happens automatically ... and you can really focus on the sound of my voice...

And now ... when you think about your sport ...

Suggestions

The simplest way of making suggestions is to be direct and give specific instructions for the improvements you want. Repeat the instruction several times throughout the hypnosis. Below is a table of various suggestions you could make:

Motivation: From now on, you will find that each day you train, the more fun you will have, and the more you train and participate in your sport, the easier you find it and the better you become, so that whenever you think about your sport and training for your sport, you are overcome with a strong desire to train, to become better and more focused.

Strength: Each time you train and compete, you will find that your muscles are stronger and more powerful. You have more force, more energy, more strength. You notice that performing tasks that were difficult becomes easier, and simpler. You notice that you have greater control, greater focus and accuracy ... That's right, and your muscles are becoming both stronger and more flexible. And you will notice too, that your recovery time after training becomes significantly faster, while your body builds just the right sort of muscle that is needed for you to compete successfully in your sport and train successfully in your sport. As your muscles become stronger and more powerful, your body is becoming healthier and stronger too, any old injuries you had heal better and faster, old weaknesses can now become strengths and your body is becoming better, healthier, more powerful and stronger...

Fear and anxiety: As you consider that fear, that you have previously experienced, you can let your

The Champion

body relax and separate fear from reality, because you know that fear is just an emotion and emotional states can be changed ... just as fear can change ... when you were little, you were probably once afraid of the dark ... but now, look at you ... you are no longer afraid ... and people sometimes want to hold onto fear, because they think that fear helps them, but if you think about it, about that fear that you had, how did it help you? Did it make you calm? Did it enable you to accurately assess the danger and to avoid it? Because, usually, people find that they deal with danger much better when they can assess danger rationally, and that they are safer and happier when they are calm ... and this means that you can now release this fear, fully and completely, release this negative emotion, let it wash away from you, filling you with calm and enabling you to rationally analyse any situation, that's right, looking after and protecting you by releasing that fear that you once had. That's right and so you can now let that fear go, let it fall into your past, forget that fear that you once had ... forget it fully and completely ... So that you are now clear headed, focused, calm ... that's right ...

Going into flow

And whenever you compete in your sport, you can now perform at your very best. Whenever competing your body can relax and your subconscious takes over. Trained reactions and responses automatically take over and you effortlessly perform at your best. And when we say, "your best" we really mean better than you ever imagined, moving fluidly, softly, powerfully, letting your intuition and subconscious mind guide you to performing better and better ... and the more you practice, the better you become ... easily going into the zone, into

The Champion

the flow of perfect performance ...

Positivity And from time to time you may have had doubts about yourself, about what you can do and whether it is worth continuing ... whether you are in the gym, or jogging or in the middle of a competition ... or relaxing after dinner in the comfort of your house ... you might sometimes have doubts... whenever such a doubt comes to you, you can feel a new burst of energy, a new sense of determination and instead of asking questions like "is it worth it?", "can I go on?", in the back of the mind you can hear a voice urging you on, "Come on, let's do this! You can do this!"... That's right ... and one of the great things about doing sport is the sense of positivity and confidence that builds within you whenever you train and compete ... and you can let this positivity flow on and beyond your sport, so it touches other elements of your life, seeping into and overwhelming other areas of your life, making you more positive, more motivated, more inspired and inspiring in your sport and in life, in general ...

Time distortion

And you know that time is relative ... And so is our perception of time ... Sometimes when you are bored, time seems to slow ... And sometimes when we are with friends, having a good time ... it seems to fly ... And you will have noticed too, after driving a car along the highway or motorway and you need to slow down ... it all seems incredibly slow ... and that means that you become accustomed to slowing fast things down ... and you can do that now ... when doing your sport, slow down the external world, so that you can respond even faster to what's happening ... That's right ... And what's more, when you are having fun,

The Champion

it makes sense to slow things down, so you can enjoy more of what you love ... that's right ...

Injury recovery

And now as you consider that injury that you received, you can leave the emotions and the disappointment behind you ... forget about the unpleasantness ... that's right ... and let your body and subconscious now focus on how quickly you can heal and recover. That's right ... because your body knows how to recover quickly and easily ... pumping additional blood to injured muscles ... sending nutrients, healing old injuries, letting the muscles relax and recover quickly ... and as you start to think about how quickly former injuries can heal, recover and strengthen, you might even notice a tingling pulsing in the muscle as the recovery begins to accelerate now ... and you might feel a warmth in your muscles, tendons and ligaments as they heal and become healthier, stronger, now recovering ... And as you think now about the injury that you received, you can now throw it out along with other unneeded junk, let any old trauma, recollections of the injury fade from your memory and disappears ... and the more you let go of that old injury now, the easier and faster your body can recover, bringing more nutrients and blood to heal and increase recovery, so that the muscle tingles and feels warm with the rapid recovery ... and you can remember how good you feel when your muscles, tendons and ligaments are in top physical condition, strong and elastic.

These are examples of the sort of language and suggestions you can use to achieve certain outcomes. A good hypnotic script will repeat suggestions in different ways. It is possible to simply loop these suggestions and that will also be beneficial but by extending such suggestions you will be more thorough and the hypnosis will often be more effective.

Concluding a hypnotic suggestion

In order to ensure that a hypnosis session will continue to have benefits after the session, be clear during hypnosis when and where the suggestions are to be applied. It sometimes happens that the benefits are only felt while the person is hypnotised, as is the case with stage hypnosis, and stage hypnotists are very careful to give instructions to make sure any suggestions given during a performance are cancelled as soon as it is over. We, on the other hand want to make sure that the suggestions are applied <u>specifically</u> for training and competition. If you have hypnotised yourself to be more aggressive in competition, make sure the instructions specify, "when I am fighting in a bout, in competition, I am much aggressive, I have higher levels of adrenalin and testosterone when fighting, as soon as the bout is over and I leave the ring/dojo, my aggression immediately fades." <u>It is important to be context specific</u> – too much aggression can get you into fights, car accidents, police cells, hospitals and morgues.

When you are concluding a hypnosis session give specific instructions: "And as you/I come out of trance, all of the changes that have been made can be applied to those occasions when they are needed ... and that these changes can be applied now on both a subconscious and conscious level, so they stay with you/me on an ongoing basis to be used and applied when training and competing in my sport."

Using anchoring to improve hypnosis

Hypnosis is a state of mind, and just as other states can be kinaesthetically or audibly anchored, so can hypnosis. This is in fact a technique which is used in some forms of Indian meditation where the guru teaches an adept to meditate. The adept is instructed to sit in a certain position (kinaesthetic anchor) and to relax while repeating to himself over and over again a mantra (auditory anchor). He does this while relaxing and going into a trance/meditative state. Once an anchor is set, the position (for example, the lotus position) and the mantra alone are sufficient to bring the adept into a meditative/trancelike state. You can use these same principles to quickly go into trance and give yourself suggestions. The technique is very simple:

1. Decide on a kinaesthetic and auditory anchor to use as your triggers. I clasp certain fingers on my left hand as a kinaesthetic anchor, and I say to myself "go into trance" as an auditory anchor, which

The Champion

also doubles as a general instruction to go into trance while I am consciously relaxing.

2. Use a hypnotic induction to go into a light trance.

3. Give your subconscious a suggestion that every time you use your chosen auditory anchor together with your kinaesthetic anchor, you will immediately go into a light trance which is receptive to suggestions you give yourself.

Peter D. Campbell

Pain relief

Pain is a natural response telling your body not to use a part of the body which is injured. Ignoring pain can lead to long term physical disabilities depending on the nature of the injury. Knowing how to deal with pain can be useful and even lifesaving, but there is always a risk and you as an athlete need to assess whether the benefits are worth the possible consequences.

Pain is a highly subjective experience. The degree to which we experience pain depends on such things as chemical balance, emotions, tiredness and attention. Most of us have had the experience of not noticing a cut or an injury until sometime after it happened. Chemicals such as adrenalin and cortisol also can suppress pain. There are battle accounts of soldiers who have lost limbs and continued fighting for extensive periods before realizing the loss.

The Champion

While such cases of natural anaesthetic occur subconsciously, it is possible to consciously harness these abilities using either hypnosis or visualization techniques.

One of the earliest uses of hypnosis was for pain relief. Dr James Esdaile, a surgeon in India in the 19th century did thousands of operations using hypnosis as an anaesthetic. On one occasion he even operated on himself. In the 20th century Dr Milton Erickson, who did much to popularize hypnosis and hypnotherapy, used to teach hypnosis to dentists so that they could anaesthetize patients hypnotically for procedures including extractions and drilling.[30]

Using hypnosis for pain relief has several advantages. Pain killers, especially in tablet form, can be harmful, while powerful pain killers can have side effects making you either drowsy, stimulated, nauseous, etc. However, the primary advantage of using hypnosis and some of the other techniques discussed here, is that if you don't have access to painkillers or if the pain

---

[30] Dr. Erickson used hypnosis and visualization techniques extensively on himself. As a teenager he contracted polio and attributes his recovery largely to visualization and self-hypnosis. In later life he contracted the disease again and used hypnosis to reduce the pain. In later years when the pain was severe, he needed to spend about an hour each morning reducing the pain before he got up.

killers you have access to aren't strong enough, there is another remedy you can use: your own mind. This is particularly useful for extreme athletes who might be hours away from any medical assistance and in some cases might have to walk out of the wilderness despite serious injury. There are several ways of removing or lessening pain using hypnosis.

1. Direct suggestion: give direct instructions that you cannot feel any pain in the area where there is pain. Emphasize the fact that the area feels comfortable and fit. Hypnotists generally think that it is better to focus on the outcome, not what you want to avoid, but sometimes giving a specific command like "you cannot feel any pain" works wonders.

2. Change the sensation: give a suggestion for the pain to be expressed in a different way, you could experience the pain as a sense of cold, or a sense of numbness. In fact, the greater the pain, the greater the numbness. This will give you an anaesthetic which becomes more powerful the stronger the pain.

3. Change the modality: pain hurts because we are experiencing it kinaesthetically. Give yourself instructions for the pain to be expressed in music, or as mosaic dance lights. This gives the body a chance to express the

pain but without the hurt. The more painful an injury the faster the music can play, or the deeper. You can also use these rhythms to enhance performance. If you play a fast beat, your body will want to move faster, in time with the music. This could potentially lead to serious injury. You can also turn the pain into music and then turn the volume down.

Other techniques for pain control

Hypnosis is not the only technique that can be used for pain control. There are other techniques which are sometimes just as effective and don't require the use of a hypnotic induction.

One of the simplest pain control techniques is to visualize the pain as an image or a symbol and then imagine burning it or sending it out into the distance. Although I have heard from endurance athletes that this technique helps, I have never found it particularly useful myself.

A more advanced technique can be an application of the parts-integration technique discussed above for dealing with self-sabotage. The technique relies on recognizing the pain, recognizing that it serves a useful purpose and then asking the part of your body generating the pain to stop generating it.

Peter D. Campbell

Parts Integration for pain control

1. Place your hands in front of you and ask the part, generating the pain to come out of you and sit/stand in your left hand. Ask yourself what does it look like? How does it feel? What temperature is it? Does it move? What size is it? People give a variety of answers, sometimes the part is large and heavy, sometimes small, sometimes it looks like them, often it looks like an unhappy version of them. In general there is a wide variety, work with whatever options come to mind. Often people don't actually "see" or "feel" the part but answers just come to mind. Work with these. Once the part has come out, thank it for appearing and being prepared to "talk" with you.

2. Ask the part of you which wants to continue what you are doing and ask it to come out of you and sit/stand in your right hand. Ask yourself what does it look like? How does it feel? What temperature is it? Does it move? What size is it? Once the part has come out, thank it for appearing and being prepared to "talk" with you.

3. Still focusing on that part in your right hand, tell it that you understand that it

The Champion

wants to help you. Ask it what its intention is? What does it want? Wait until some answer appears in your mind. Often it will appear to be extremely simple and prosaic.

4. Once you have the answer, ask it to imagine that it has that has that intention completely and fully, and having that intention completely and fully, ask it what it wants which is even more important. Wait until an answer comes to mind.

5. Continue asking this question. As you receive answers and reiterate the question you will find yourself going through a list of wants and desires that represent the sort of person you are. Often when people finally reach the end of the iteration, they find that what they really want is happiness, peace, love, or a sense of oneness or wholeness. Once you have reached the final iteration ...

6. Turn your attention to the part, which is in your left hand, and tell it that you understand that it wants to help you. Ask it what it is trying to achieve through the pain (which you perceive as self-sabotage), ask it what its intention is. Wait until some answer appears in your mind. Often it will appear to be extremely simple and prosaic.

7. Once you have the answer, ask it to imagine that it has that intention completely and fully, and ask it what it wants which is even more important. Wait until an answer comes to mind.

8. Continue asking this question until you start getting the same answers as you received for your right hand. This demonstrates to both parts that they have the same goals and aims and are simply working against each other to try to achieve them. Ask the part in the left hand if it recognizes this? Usually, it will. Sometimes it won't, in which case you need to continue following the intentions further until you reach the identical highest intention (peace, calm, etc).

9. When the two parts have agreed that they share the same intentions ask them if they can now work together to achieve the same goals. Often, at this point the left hand will be reluctant because it has very good reasons (as it perceives them) for making you feel the pain. You can then ask it what it needs in order to cooperate with your right hand. This is where you need to start negotiations and often your right hand will

The Champion

need to agree to some of the needs of the left hand.

10. Conduct the negotiations between the hand asking each what it wants and what it needs. They usually come to an agreement quite quickly.

11. Having agreed the two parts can then recognize that they can work together you can then place your hands together. When they do come together people often see the parts merging and becoming a single representation. You can then let this united, single part, return to your body.

Changing the pain

Pain is an imprecise term. Often when we talk about pain we fail to specify what the sensation actually is. Research into pain indicates that the more emotions associated with the experience the more painful it is. Many people when they receive an injury exaggerate its significance. A fracture, in their imagination, becomes a lifelong disability; a ligament injury means that they will never run again, etc. By focusing on the physical symptoms, and focusing only on the immediate problem, you can reduce the experience of pain. It also enables you to analyse whether the injury is serious enough to stop you from training or competing.

However, there is more to pain than the emotions associated with it. Pain is a message that is transferred to our brains, our brains receive electrical input and interpret it as hurting and generates that pain. This means that we can deliberately alter the representation of pain.

Altering representation of pain

1. Ask yourself a series of questions:
    a. Where is the pain?
    b. What shape is the pain?
    c. What colour is the pain?
    d. Is the pain moving? If so how is it moving? Is it pulsating, spinning, throbbing?
    e. Is it a sharp pain or dull pain?
    f. Is it hot or cold?
2. Change the severity of the pain. Initially try making the pain hurt more to demonstrate to yourself that it is possible to use your imagination to change the degree of pain you experience. Now, imagine the pain as being less painful.

The Champion

3. Start altering some of these pain properties. This is a process of experimentation, some changes will reduce the pain, others will intensify the pain. Experiment and find which representations give you greatest pain relief.

4. Often people depict pain as being a jagged object, sharp and pointed. Experiment, and see if you can alter the shape of the pain from something sharp and pointed to something soft and round. Notice how this alters your perception of the sensations.

5. Change the colour of the pain. Often people represent pain as being red, change it to a soothing green, or blue. Some people like to change the pain to gold or silver (colours often associated with love). Try using different colours and notice what difference it makes to your experience of the sensations.

6. Change how the pain is moving. If the pain is still, try moving it in a certain direction. If it is moving, make it move in the opposite direction, or make it sit still in one position. Notice how this alters the way you experience the sensations.

7. Change the temperature of the pain. Cool it down or increase the temperature and notice the difference it makes.

8. Change where the pain is located. You can now experiment moving the pain around your body. If you have abdominal pain, move it to another part of the abdomen. If you have knee pain, move it up into your thigh or down into your calf.

These experiments will show you that you can alter how you experience pain and can consciously alter the experience of that pain. Once you have found the most comfortable representations of pain you can use these to deliberately improve how you feel. As a final step, having experimented with different representations of pain, when you start changing the location of the pain, imagine the pain now departing your body, once you are visualising the pain outside your body, its painfulness is further reduced and sometimes disappears entirely.

Final notes on pain control

Pain control is a skill and not simply a matter of gritting your teeth and bearing it until it disappears. As with most skills it can take time and practice to master. Such skills can be highly

The Champion

useful for some athletes, for others it is less relevant. However, if you do find that you are in pain and either cannot take pain killers or don't want to, these techniques can be practised. As pain often hinders injury recovery, these techniques can also be useful. The key is to experiment with different pain control techniques and practice those that come most easily to you.

Peter D. Campbell

Altering perceptions of reality

Our perception of reality affects how easy it is for us to achieve tasks. Often perceptions are nothing more than self-fulfilling prophecies (as discussed in the section on Beliefs). Many of the techniques in this book work by altering our subconscious perceptions of reality establishing new or different associations and training our brain to respond in accordance with these altered perceptions.

The following information is based on accounts given by both Anthony Robbins and Dr. Richard Bandler. In their seminars they refer to work they carried out in the 1980s for the US military in which they claim to have constructed a mental template of the ideal soldier. For example, according to Bandler and Robbins good snipers will subconsciously bring the target closer to them, so that on a subconscious level they appear to be shooting at something located at close range instead of long range. They emphasise that this is something that golfers do as well.

So, if this is true, how do you alter your subconscious perception of reality? If you could alter reality to make your sport easier, what would you do?

Both Bandler and Robbins tell nearly identical stories about coaching professional baseball players. They get the baseball player to imagine the baseball as being really big, and floating slowly through the air, much like a balloon – something that you can't miss. They get them to repeat this visualisation several times.

This technique seems absurdly simply but as it is quick to do, it is worth trying. Personally, I do not understand how or why it works. Common sense would have it that the more accurate our perception of reality is, the more useful. However, this concept has been used successfully by athletes and I have used it for fencing and would recommend that athletes at least experiment with it to see if it is beneficial.

Altering subconscious perception

1. Think of a skill that you would like to improve. A basketball player might like to make shooting for the net easier, a soccer or hockey player might want to make

shooting for goal easier, a bowler at cricket might want to make it easier to bowl a batsman out, a runner might want to make long distances easier to run, etc.

2. Once you know what you want to make easier, think of what would make that skill easier. Usually this involves making the target or the goal bigger, so if you are a hockey player wanting to make it easier to score a goal, you imagine a large goal, which is impossible to miss. If you are a goalie, you might want to increase your own size and decrease the size of the goal so that it is easier to protect. Archers and target shooters can imagine the target being closer and larger. For fencing, I imagine competitors with large target areas and very short arms. A tennis player might like to increase the size of the opponent's court and decrease the size of the opponent and his/her own court, so it is perceived as being easier to defend.

3. Once you have an image you want to use, visualise competing and training with the new representations, seeing yourself striking the target (or achieving whatever skill you want to achieve) easily, over and over again.

The Champion

4. After you have spent some time (maybe a minute or so) visualising point 3, let your mind go blank. Think about something completely different for maybe half a minute (think about going for a walk, what you want to do on the weekend, when you get home, etc.) Then repeat the visualisation. Do this seven times. The more you do it, the more effective this should be, but seven times is sufficient to get some benefit from the exercise.

5. Go out and test how well this has worked.

Peter D. Campbell

Training diaries

Most coaches recommend that you keep a training diary. The main use of a training diary is to plan and record your activities so that training is focussed and consistent with your needs. However, a diary can provide all sorts of additional information and is particularly easy to maintain now as a computer spreadsheets.

The more information you keep in a training diary the more you can manage your training scientifically. Suggested information could be:

1. Goals: include your long term and short term goals and what skills, physical fitness and strength you need to acquire to achieve them. This should be a mini-training plan.

2. Resting pulse in the morning: If your resting pulse jumps dramatically it means you are overtraining. Reduce your training until your pulse returns to its normal rate.

3. Amount of sleep: this might help explain tiredness and weakness.

4. General exercise: What exercises you are doing, push-ups, sit-ups (repetitions and sets), runs (distance, times).

5. Diet: What you are eating, number of calories, amount of protein, health supplements.

6. Health: how you feel, energy levels, muscle recovery.

7. Sport specific training: technical training you are doing, one or two areas for improvement, five things that you are doing well. Which aspects of the game most need remedial attention?

By maintaining a detailed training diary, you can work out why things go well and why they go wrong. Furthermore, by focusing on one or two things that require improvement, you will steadily improve your performance. By noting five things that you do well, you will constantly reinforce the fact that there are things you do well. This keeps you positive which helps with motivation, and also helps in increasing the speed with which you learn. Confident and happy people learn significantly faster than demoralised people.

Peter D. Campbell

Video recording

Video recording is an effective addition to your training diary. Most people have access to some form of video recorder whether it is a camera or a telephone and most are sufficient for the task.

Take regular videos of your performance and keep them on record. After training or competition you can review the video to see what you did wrong, but more importantly what you did right. I find that when I compete I can normally list a dozen or so things that I did wrong, I am much less aware of all the things I got right, unless they were extremely good. The video captures everything and watching it can be a rewarding experience.

Furthermore, a video library becomes a useful reference. You can review what you were doing six months before and compare it with what you are doing now. You can see improvements in your performance. If for some reason your performance has deteriorated you can refer to the video, analyse it and see what you were doing differently when you were getting better results.

The Champion

Competition

If you are training for a competitive sport, all training is competition preparation. It is helpful to plan in advance what competitions you will participate in, what results you want to achieve in each competition and how you need to train to achieve those results. Know what you can reasonably achieve and aim a little bit higher. Then focus training on elements that will enable you to achieve that higher level. This should include elements already discussed:

- fitness and strength training,
- mental rehearsal,
- technical skills training.

Depending on where you are at the training cycle you might emphasise different areas of training. For example, if fitness has been letting you down in past competitions, you might focus more on aerobic training. If you have good technique but are slow, you will want to develop speed while maintaining good technique; this might require specific strength training to increase speed, or might simply be a matter of repeating the action numerous times to train the muscles (and the brain) to perform the action quickly and correctly. Developing speed without proper technique will simply lead to difficulties down the track and will require retraining. It is easier and in the long run quicker to train to do things the right way.

About two weeks from competition focus primarily on the techniques which you think are important for competition. This will usually be <u>basic</u> technique, the fundamentals for your sport and those techniques which you intend to use most. This period is largely revision.

In terms of physical training, about a week or ten days before competition do an intensive training session to really tire you. This helps to acclimatize the body to extreme physical activity, it also will make you take the next few days off to recover. This is useful in helping prevent you from overtraining in the final days before the competition.

Take a couple of days to recover from the intensive training session. Spend some time doing mental rehearsal. When doing the mental

The Champion

rehearsal focus on the approaching tournament. The more specific you can make such visualisations the better: you know the venue imagine yourself competing there. If you know your competition, see yourself at the venue competing defeating your main opponents. The more you know of their technique, the more specific you can make these mental rehearsals. For example, if you know that your main opponent uses an unusual style, see yourself using techniques to defeat that style. If you do not know your competition so well, see yourself competing against them focusing on your strong points and seeing yourself beat them. If you have no idea who your competition is, focus on what you do well and see yourself competing successfully against various people. Mentally rehearse countering techniques that you have found difficult, and mentally practise as many aspects of your sport as possible so that you are psychologically ready. Training psychologically as well as physically will enable you to mentally prepared competition day.

Exercise during the last week, and particularly the day before competition presents sportspeople with a difficulty decision about how to exercise and train. Some exercise and training is clearly essential but how much and for how long? There are two generally accepted approaches and their success depends more on the athlete than the approach. One approach is to go for short high intensity training, which can be done quickly and so doesn't tire the athlete. However, the higher intensity does increase potential risk of injury because it places the body under greater stress. The other approach is to do longer, low intensity training, which places less stress on the body. Low intensity training can leave a sportsperson feeling tired, and can also lead to injuries associated with fatigue. In both cases, the main aim is to ensure some form of physical and technical training is carried out without risking over-fatigue or injury. By focusing at this stage more on mental rehearsal you can reduce the risk of injury.

During the build up to the competition make sure that equipment is brought into order and that you have spares of everything you need. Check travel arrangements and arrange for food throughout the competition. The more things that are prepared in advance the less likely you are to be distracted from the competition. Additional stress on the day of the competition can be very off-putting. During your competition the fewer distractions you have the better.

Nutrition

A few days (up to four days) before the competition start loading carbohydrates. Carbohydrates are essential to fuel your body and pre-loading will give you more energy for competition day. While quantity is important, what is more important is quality. These carbohydrates should have a low glycemic index, meaning that the energy is released slowly into your body. Such carbohydrates include rice (brown rice is particularly good), potatoes and whole grains, dense "brown" bread not highly refined, soft "white" bread which is little better than sugar. Avoid highly processed forms such as potato chips or fries. The night before a competition have a meal of about 1,000 calories. The day of the competition have another meal of about 800 calories two hours before competition. My trainer recommended a meal of 3,000 calories the day of the competition. While this large intake gives you plenty of energy to keep you going throughout the day, it requires digesting and can slow you down rather than speed you up. When competing it is good to start the day with low glucose index food to provide for sustained effort, and then eat high glucose index food during competition, such as chocolates, various sweets, energy drinks, etc., to maintain high intensity effort. When competing you should eat about 60 grams of carbohydrates every 60-90 minutes and ensure you stay hydrated. During the final build up and the competition eat food which you are familiar with, which you can be certain will not upset your stomach or make you sick. On competition day avoid high fat foods as these slow down the digestive system.

Competition day

Arrive at the competition venue with plenty of time to avoid the stress of potentially being late. After you have gone through the administration or formality that begins a competition, start preparing.

1. If you are not in your sports clothes, get changed and get everything ready for competition.

2. Then spend some time deep breathing and relaxing, now is a good time to listen to music which relaxes you.

3. Mental rehearse how you want to perform for the day. Quickly go over the execution of basic techniques and then visualise yourself competing and doing well, achieving your goal for the competition.

The Champion

4. Use visualisation and anchors throughout the competition to keep employing the best techniques.. There is little use in having these techniques if you do not plan to use them. If you don't actively plan to use them, you are likely to forget about them during the competition.

5. Warm up, get your pulse up to 145 by doing sprints, using a skipping rope, etc.

6. Practice session. If you do a martial art, spar with someone, wake your reactions up and get your eye in. The same applies for hand-and-eye sports such as tennis and cricket. Activate your anchors to put you in the correct mental state.

7. Before every bout/fight/heat/game visualise your intended performance. If you play a sport such as golf or croquet, visualise what you are going today before each turn. Visualise every stroke before taking it.

8. Before every bout/fight/heat/game raise your heartrate to about 130 beats per minute.

9. Maintain control of emotions. Throughout the competition maintain a good and positive state of mind. Use anchoring

techniques to stay focused, control your internal dialogue. <u>Use encouraging language</u>. It is important to do this both while competing and while you have down time.

10.   Maintain fluids and energy. Eat about 60 grams of carbohydrates every hour.

Winning

Winners are able to control their emotions and focus solely on the present. The most common distractions are:

- Weather conditions: temperature, wind, rain, and sun;
- Opponent: domineering or intimidating behaviour, reputation, fake injuries, jeers/jokes/comments;
- Spectators: behaviour, comments whether supportive or hostile can distract you;
- Self: hunger, fatigue, pain, injuries;
- Self: your emotions, hopes, fears and self-talk dramatically affect performance.

Much of the preparation and visualization covered in this book is designed to enable you to ignore distractions and stay focused.

The Champion

Any athlete who is being distracted during competition should take the following steps:

- Breathe: slow your breathing down, calm yourself and refocus;
- Identify the emotion: being able to name the emotion re-engages your analytical mind and helps break you out of negative mental state.
- Anchor: use your pre-set anchors to bring you back into the right frame of mind to compete;
- Talk to yourself: use language which is positive and encouraging to refocus on the present
- Visualize: use an appropriate visualization technique to bring yourself back into the game. This might involve simply visualizing your next serve or the next point, or it might involve using the masking technique.

What happens when you are competing and everything starts going much better than expected? You might have aimed for placing around tenth in a competition and suddenly it looks like you might come in the top three? How do you respond? You get another shot of adrenalin, butterflies suddenly flutter in your stomach and your arms which were steady as steel a moment before start shaking. How do you stay focused?

Controlled breathing, anchoring and visualization are a good start. Deep breathing and anchoring is helpful in any situation but often athletes still find themselves distracted by thoughts about winning, what it will feel like, and even see themselves on the winner's podium whereas they need to be thinking about the here and now, focusing on the present.

Once you have a moment to pull yourself together, allow your mind to enjoy the possibility of winning. Visualize the winning ceremony, visualize any of the ideas which keep coming to you and distracting you. Make them as real as possible. After doing this visualization 'place' it somewhere out of the way, where it won't distract you. This might mean tucking it away with your sports equipment or at the end of the track. Then focus on the present, the current game/bout/fight. Make sure you keep yourself well fed, well hydrated and focused.

If, on the other hand you are too confident, you can similarly lose focus and fail to pay sufficient attention to your game. Overconfidence, in some ways, is harder to detect than a lack of confidence

The Champion

or fear. If you notice yourself thinking "this will be easy", you might be overconfident.

- Take a deep breath.
- Remember that upsets happen constantly in sport.
- Raise your pulse by jogging on the spot, skipping etc. An increased heartrate will help fire adrenaline which will keep you focused.
- Do mental rehearsals of what you need to do, focusing on staying focused, being in the zone, and beating your competition.
- Use your competitive anchors

Peter D. Campbell

Conclusion: putting it all together

Being successful at a high level in sport requires dedication. You need to be fit, strong, technically good, and in many sports, fast. Furthermore, you have to have the mental mind-set and preparation to be able to perform. All of these skills can be developed – but if not all of them come naturally you need to have a plan to develop them all, in a logical, coherent and systematic manner.

In summary an ideal athlete should on a **daily basis**:

- Practice relaxation and visualisation;
- Do technical training;
- Maintain training diary.

On a **weekly basis**:

- Do strength training at least once a week and preferably more like 3-5 times per week;

The Champion

- Do aerobic training 3-5 times per week.

A **training session** should consist of:

1. Relaxation (tactical breathing)
2. Visualisation
3. Running (increase pulse to 145)
4. Training session
5. Stretching
6. Visualisation (review)
7. Conclude training by doing something enjoyable.

The elements to success condensed in this manner are reasonably simple, however, the devil is in the detail – knowing how to use training techniques and visualisation to achieve high performance results is difficult. This book has provided you with solutions for most questions that will arise as part of your sporting career.

If you want additional advice, or other ideas to help you with your sporting career, you can book a session with the author at peter.campbell@mind-design.co.nz.

Peter D. Campbell

Appendix 1: Exercise Tables

Basic exercise plan

	Week 1	Week 2	Week 3	Week 4
Push-ups	10	13	16	20
Full squats	10	13	16	20
Pull ups	3	5	8	10
Sit-ups	10	13	16	20
Dips	10	13	16	20
Lifting exercise	10	13	16	20

The Champion

Military fitness plan for beginners

Basic training plan provided by the New Zealand Army for potential recruits to improve their fitness prior to joining. Exercise four to five times a week.

	Wk 1	Wk 2	Wk 3	Wk 4	Wk 5	Wk 6
Run	20 min	25 min 3x/wk,	30 min 2x/wk,	35 min 2x/wk	40 min 2x/wk	45 min 2x/wk
		1.6 km/9 min 2x/wk	2.4 km/12.5 min 2x/wk,	2.4 km/11.5 min 1x/wk,	2.4 km/11 min 2x/wk,	3.2 km/13.5 min 1x/wk
			1.6 km/8 min 1x/wk	1.6 km/7 min 2x/wk	2.4 km/14 min 1x/wk	2.4 km/11 min 2x/wk
Push-ups	10	16	20	24	26	28
Sit-ups	20	30	40	50	55	60
Squats	14	22	26	28	28	30
Back arches	10	14	18	20	20	20
Pull ups	3	4	5	6	8+	8+

Military fitness standards

The following military standards for fitness are included here to give the athlete a general baseline for the level of fitness expected by various military units. They can serve as a baseline to measure yourself against and can be used as general goals.

New Zealand Army fitness standards

While this information is New Zealand specific, most militaries have similar tests and this provides a good bench-mark to compare your own fitness.

Recruit

	2.4 km run	Curl-ups	Press ups
Male	12 min	45	15
Female	14 min	35	8

Grade 2 Fitness

Grade 2 fitness is what you need to achieve to graduate recruit training.

	2.4 km run	Curl-ups	Press ups
Male	10:30 min	60	28
Female	12:20 min	50	14

The Champion

Grade 1 Fitness

Grade 1 is the desired fitness level for all serving soldiers and officers in the New Zealand Army.

	2.4 km run	Curl-ups	Press ups
Male	10:00 min	66	30
Female	11:50 min	55	15

THE '100 CLUB' is the fitness level that all New Zealand Army officers and soldiers aspire to reach.

The 100 Club

	2.4 km run	Curl-ups	Press ups
Male	8:00 min	130	55
Female	10:05 min	118	36

US Navy SEALS entry requirements

	Minimum	Competitive
500 yard swim	12:30 min	8 min
Push-ups	50	80-100
Sit-ups	50	80-100
Pull ups	10	15-20

| 2.4 km run | 10:30 min | 9-10 min |

US Ranger recommended scores

Ranger PFT	Recommended Scores
Push-ups in 2:00	80
Sit-ups in 2:00	80
Pull-ups	12
Two-mile run	Sub 13:00
5 Mile run	35:00
16-mile hike w/65lb pack	4-5 hours
15-meter swim with gear	Pass/Fail

SAS in camp regime

Former SAS Sergeant Andy McNab recalled a typical training circuit that the troopers used when killing time on overseas assignments in his book *Immediate Action*. Comprising:

- Warm up run
- 2 min on punching bag
- 2 min skipping
- 2 min rest break
- 2 min weights
- 2 min skipping
- 2 min rest

Repeat circuit 10 times. Complete with warm down jog. The entire workout takes a little over two hours.

The Champion

This work out is comparable with the training world class athletes undertake on a regular basis, and in some cases exceeds it. In addition to aerobic, anaerobic, strength and endurance training, athletes will also spend time **every day** training specific sport related skills.

Peter D. Campbell

Basic Running plan

Running material taken from http://www.military.com/military-fitness/workouts/different-levels-of-running

Wk	Mon	Tues	Wed	Thu	Fri
1	1-2 miles	Bike or swim	1-2 miles	Bike or swim	1-2 miles
2	2-3 miles	Bike or swim	2-3 miles	Bike or swim	2-3 miles
3*	Bike or swim	Bike or swim	Bike or swim	Bike or swim	Bike or swim
4	3 miles	Bike or swim	3 miles	Bike or swim	3 miles
5	2 miles	3 miles	Rest day	4 miles	2 miles
6	2-3 miles	3-4 miles	Rest day	4-5 miles	2-3 miles

Do not run during Week 3 - as there is a high risk of injury. Bike or swim everyday instead.

The following nine weeks will take you to a level where you can start to train for a marathon. Just climbing to this level of running could cause tendonitis and other joint pains due to the harshness of running on the body. It is not recommended to start Running Plan II until you can perform week six from the Running Plan I.

The Champion

Intermediate Running plan

Week	Mon	Tue	Wed	Thu	Fri	Sat
1	3 miles	5 miles	Rest	3 miles	5 miles	2 miles
2	3 miles	5 miles	Rest	3 miles	5 miles	2 miles
3	4 miles	5 miles	Rest	6 miles	4 miles	3 miles
4	4 miles	5 miles	Rest	6 miles	4 miles	3 miles
5	5 miles	5 miles	Rest	6 miles	4 miles	4 miles
6	5 miles	6 miles	Rest	6 miles	6 miles	4 miles
7	6 miles	6 miles	Rest	6 miles	6 miles	6 miles
8	6 miles	6 miles	Rest	6 miles	6 miles	6 miles
9	6 miles	6 miles	Rest	6 miles	6 miles	6 miles

Work on speed and goal pace during Weeks 8-9 (minutes/mile).

Once you have the foundation of running thirty miles per week, you are now ready to train at your goal mile time and distance. Usually Saturday and Sunday make the best days for your longer run so Monday and Friday will be off days in order to recover and prepare. The chart below is a 12 week plan for a marathon:

Peter D. Campbell

Twelve Week Running Plan for Marathon Performance - Advanced Runners

Week	Tue	Wed	Thu	Sat	Sun
1	8	5	6	6	6
2	8	6	6	7	7
3	9	6	6	8	8
4	9	6	6	10	6
5	10	6	6	12	6
6	11	6	6	14	6
7	12	6	6	16	6
8	12	6	6	18	6
9	12	6	6	19	6
10	10	6	6	20	6
11	8	6	6	10	6
12	6	6	Rest	2	Marathon

Mondays and Fridays are rest days

Goal Paces:

10:00 / mile = approx. 4.5 hours

9:00 / mile = approx. 4 hours

8:00 / mile = approx. 3.5 hours

7:00 / mile = approx. 3 hours

6:00 / mile = approx. 2.5 hours

The Champion

Beep Test Levels

Information taken from "Multi-stage fitness test" at *Wikipedia.org*.

Lev	Laps	Cumulative laps	Speed (km/h)	Lap time (s)	Level time (s)	Level distance (m)	Cumulative distance (m)	Cumulative time (mm:ss)
1	8	8	8.5	8.47	67.76	160	160	1:08
2	8	16	9	8	64	160	320	2:12
3	8	24	9.5	7.58	60.63	160	480	3:12
4	9	33	10	7.2	64.8	180	660	4:17
5	9	42	10.5	6.86	61.71	180	840	5:19
6	10	52	11	6.55	65.45	200	1040	6:24
7	10	62	11.5	6.26	62.61	200	1240	7:27
8	10	72	12	6	60	200	1440	8:27
9	11	83	12.5	5.76	63.36	220	1660	9:30
10	11	94	13	5.54	60.92	220	1880	10:31
11	12	106	13.5	5.33	64	240	2120	11:35
12	12	118	14	5.14	61.71	240	2360	12:37
13	13	131	14.5	4.97	64.55	260	2620	13:42
14	13	144	15	4.8	62.4	260	2880	14:44
15	13	157	15.5	4.65	60.39	260	3140	15:44
16	14	171	16	4.5	63	280	3420	16:47
17	14	185	16.5	4.36	61.09	280	3700	17:48
18	15	200	17	4.24	63.53	300	4000	18:52
19	15	215	17.5	4.11	61.71	300	4300	19:54
20	15	230	18	4	60	300	4600	20:54
21	16	246	18.5	3.89	62.27	320	4920	21:56

Peter D. Campbell
Organisations' beep test levels

Organization	Country	Minimum level attained
Western Australian Rugby Union Referees	Australia	10.5 (Premier Grade), 9.5 (Reserve Grade)
Rugby Football referee	England (RFU)	10.4 for development squads, 12+ for elite referees
British Army Officer	UK	10.2 (male), 8.1 (female)
Royal Air Force	UK	9.10 (male), 7.2 (female)
Royal Air Force Regiment	UK	11.7 (male)
Royal Marines	UK	13 Marine, 15 Officer
Airservices Australia	Australia	9.6
Metropolitan Fire Brigade (Melbourne)	Australia	9.6
Fire and Rescue NSW	Australia	9.6 (Permanents) 8.7 (Retained/Part Timers)
Royal Military College of Canada	Canada	9.5 (male), 7.5 (female)
Scottish Police	UK	9.2 (male), 7.3 (female) (aged 18–29) - 15 Metre shuttle only
South Australia Police	Australia	9.04 (male), 6.10 (female)
Queensland Fire and Rescue Service	Australia	8.7
Western Australia Police	Australia	8.1 to 10.1+ (male), 6.1 to 7.1 (female)

The Champion

Australian Army	Australia	7.5
Australian Special Forces	Australia	10.1
New Zealand Defence Forces	New Zealand	Navy : 6.1 Airforce : 7.1 Army : 8.8
French Foreign Legion	France	7
Royal Australian Navy	Australia	6.9 to 7.4
Royal Australian Air Force	Australia	6.5
Australian Federal Police	Australia	6.5
Ontario Provincial Police	Canada	6.5
Queensland Police Service	Australia	6.3 to 9.4 (male), 5.1 to 7.5 (female)
Canadian Forces	Canada	6.0 (male), 4.0 (female) (under 35)
English and Welsh Police	UK	5.4 (general roles) to 10.5
Victoria Police	Australia	5.1 (updated 23/7/2012 to new standards)
New South Wales Police Force	Australia	7.1
Blue Bulls Rugby Referee Association	South Africa	9.9 for entry level qualification

Peter D. Campbell

Appendix 2: Diet and nutrition

Nutritional information originally sourced from the New Zealand Academy of Sport in 2008.

Daily protein requirements

Athletes	Grams/kg of body weight
Inactive	0.8-1
Elite endurance	1.6
Recreational endurance	0.8-1
Football, power sports	1.4–1.7
Resistance, early training	1.5–1.7
Resistance, steady training	1.0–1.2

Protein requirements for female athletes

Women require 15% less protein then men, so protein requirements for women athletes are as follows:

Female athlete	50 kg	55 kg	60 kg	65 kg	70 kg
Inactive	40-50 g	44-55 g	48-60 g	52-65 g	56-70 g

The Champion

Elite endurance	68 g	75 g	82 g	88 g	95 g
Recreational endurance	40-50 g	44-55 g	48-60 g	52-65 g	56-70 g
Football, power sports	60-72 g	66-79 g	71-87 g	77-94 g	83-101 g
Resistance, early training	64-72 g	70-79 g	77-87 g	83-94 g	89-101 g
Resistance, steady training	43-51 g	47-56 g	51-61 g	55-66 g	60-71 g

Protein requirements for male athletes

Male athlete	70 kg	75 kg	80 kg	85 kg	90 kg
Inactive	56-70	60-75	64-80	68-85	72-90
Elite endurance	112	120	128	136	144
Recreational endurance	56-70	60-75	64-80	68-85	72-90
Football, power sports	98-119	105-128	112-136	119-145	126-153
Resistance, early training	105-119	113-128	120-136	128-145	135-153
Resistance, steady training	70-84	75-90	80-96	85-102	90-108

Protein counting

Food	Serve size	Protein in grams
Meats		
Beef/lamb/pork	100 g	31 g
Ham/salami	1 slice	7 g
Sausage	1 cooked	13 g
Chicken/turkey	100 g	28 g
Seafood flesh	100 g	23 g
Dairy Food		
Milk	250 ml	9 g
Cheese	20 g slice	5 g
Cottage cheese	1 tbsp	3 g
Yoghurt	200 g	10 g
Ice cream	1 scoop	2 g
Grains		
Rice	1 cup	5 g
Pasta	1 cup	5 g
Breads	1 slice	3 g
Breakfast cereals	30-45 g	3-5 g
Vegetable/fruit		
Potato	1 medium	3.5 g
Boiled corn	1 cup	2 g
Banana	1 medium	1.5 g
Tinned fruit	1 cup	1 g

The Champion

Avocado	1 medium	2 g
Miscellaneous		
Eggs	1 cooked	7 g
Tofu	100 g	8.5 g
Baked beans	1 cup	10 g
Nuts	50 g	10 g

Carbohydrates

Daily Carbohydrate requirements for regular training (4-7 days per week)

Training intensity	Grams of carbohydrates per kg of body weight
Low intensity sports (bowls, croquet, shooting)	Basic nutritional needs provides sufficient carbohydrates. Although pre-training and post-training snacks are still necessary.
Up to 60 minutes of moderate to high intensity training daily (golf)	5-6 g/kg
60-120 minutes of moderate to high intensity training (sprint training, rugby, hockey, football, racquet sports, throwing sports, sailing, rowing, strength and lifting sports, short triathlons)	7-8 g/kg
Endurance training (2-5 hours intense training a day (distance running, cycling, swimming)	9-10 g/kg
Extreme training, more than 5 hours training per day (ironman, multisport	10 g/kg

The Champion

endurance events, ultra running)

Snacks for recovery after training

55kg Athlete	Snack	Carbohydrates
Option One	Sports drink 500 ml	35 g
	1 muffin	20 g
Total		55 g
Option Two		
	1 roll with banana	55 g
75kg Athlete	**Snack**	**Carbohydrates**
Option One	Sports drink 500 ml	35 g
	1 white roll with honey	30 g
	10 jet planes	10 g
Total		75 g
Option Two		
	Sports drink 500ml	35 g

	2 slices of bread with jam	30 g
	1 fruit	10-15 g
Total		75-80 g
85kg Athlete	**Snack**	**Carbohydrates**
Option One	Sports drink 500 ml	35 g
	2 slices of bread/rolls	25 g
	1 banana/2 fruit	25 g
Total		85 g
Option Two		
	Sports drink 500ml	35 g
	1 cereal bar	30 g
	2 fruit	25 g
Total		85 g

The Champion

Calories

To find out how many calories you need to support your sport it is best to find a calculator online, which can give you a precise figure. However, the following table will give you a general idea of how much you should be eating.

Calorie needs

Height (cm)	Light activity	Moderate activity	Heavy activity
150	1455-1920	1649-2176	1940-2560
155	1560-2040	1768-2312	2080-2720
160	1650-2175	1870-2465	2200-2900
165	1770-2325	2006-2635	2360-3100
170	1875-2460	2125-2788	2500-3280
175	1980-2610	2244-2958	2640-3480
180	2100-2760	2380-3128	2800-3680
185	2220-2910	2516-3298	2960-3880

Peter D. Campbell

Recommended dietary intake

Recommended dietary intake by US government broken into protein, fat and carbohydrates.

High-Protein diet

	Protein	Fat	Carbohydrate
Calories	30%	30%	40%
2000	600 cal	600 cal	800 cal
	150 g	67 g	200 g

Low Carbohydrate Weight-loss Diet

	Protein	Fat	Carbohydrate
Calories	25%	65%	10%
2000	500 cal	1300 cal	200 cal
	125 g	144 g	50 g

	Protein	Fat	Carbohydrate
Calories	25%	65%	10%
1800	450 cal	1170 cal	180 cal
	113 g	130 g	45 g

The Champion

U.S. Government Recommended Diet

	Protein	Fat	Carbohydrate
Calories	15%	30%	55 %
2000	300 cal	600 cal	1100 cal
	75 g	67 g	275 g

Appendix 3: Visualisation Techniques

Installing anchors

Step 1: To install an anchor firstly you need to decide what action you want to use as the trigger. This needs to be an action that you can easily perform while doing your sport. For sport I have a range of anchors which I can use with my left hand and consist of holding my fingers in set, unnatural positions (so I don't use the anchors accidentally). I have trained divers who have chosen to use the "All OK" sign as a trigger to relax them. I worked with one corporate executive who chose to hold his wrist in a certain way, which he could do inconspicuously at meetings, to control nervousness (and sometimes anger). Other sportspeople I have worked with have used triggers such as holding an ear between their thumb and forefinger. I had a client who had subconsciously set up an anchor by stroking his hair. Choose an appropriate trigger for yourself appropriate to the demands of your sport. Maintaining various holds, or applying pressure to particular parts of the body work best as they give the body time to adjust to the physiological changes that need to take place.

Step 2: Decide on the state you want to anchor. Athletes usually choose to create separate anchors for each state they want to use when competing. A state of calm is often used before a bout, fight, penalty shot, etc. to enable the sportsperson to focus on the current task and take control of nerves, fear, or excess energy. A state of flow is usually triggered after the athlete has achieved calmness, and is used to place him/her in that state in which performance comes easily and comfortably. A 'psyched–up' or alert state is usually only useful if you are going to do something that requires large release of physical energy. Weight lifters might want to psyche themselves up before a big lift; boxers and martial artists will want to psyche themselves up for particularly aggressive opponents. I have personally only deliberately psyched myself up once for an epée bout and that was against an opponent who was more aggressive than I, and who was accustomed to being the most aggressive person on the piste. I wanted to turn the tables on him and needed to psych myself up, to force him to fight on my terms not his. For most sports being calm or in flow is a more productive state. However, psyching can be used if you are underperforming because you are not getting an adrenaline rush.

Step 3: Go into the state you want to anchor. This is achieved by remembering a time when you felt the desired state. Remember the experience in careful detail, remember what was happening, remember what you were doing, what you did, remember how you felt, remember what you heard, what you saw and cast yourself back into that experience.

Step 4: Apply the trigger. Once you feel that you are fully re-living the experience, apply the trigger which you have already decided on. While continuing to apply the trigger, continue also to experience the state which you want to anchor. Hold this for about 30 seconds to a minute. By establishing a unique trigger when you are in the desired state you create an association between the trigger and the state, so that in the future, when you use the trigger, it triggers the state – just like Pavlov's dogs salivating when they heard the bell.

Step 5: Strengthening the anchor. Once is enough to establish an anchor, but it never hurts to practice it. Deliberately apply the anchor several times a day and while applying it go through the entire process described in step 3. When you are naturally in the desired state, apply the trigger again, just to strengthen the association.

Anchoring is a powerful technique, and is often something which can be done in a few minutes. When giving demonstrations to athletes, or asked at a dinner party for a tip to improve sports performance, I usually teach anchoring. However, it is not always easy to go into the necessary state. For example some sportspeople might have had only a few fleeting experiences of being "in flow" so recreating that state can be difficult. It is something that might need practice and effort to achieve. If you cannot get into the state of flow, keep on trying, but establish anchors for being relaxed and ready, rather than in flow. The flow will come with time.

To create an anchor

1. Choose the trigger
2. Choose the state you want to anchor
3. Go into the desired state
4. Activate the trigger

Strengthen the anchor

Peter D. Campbell

Potterat's recipe for resilience:
1. Focus on the present
2. Imagine how good it will feel
3. Breathe deeply
4. Cheer yourself on

Trauma recovery:

The following mental rehearsal enables you to dramatically reduce psychological trauma. It may seem strangely metaphysical but the technique is designed to dissociate you from the events. Read over the exercise first so that you know what to expect and then do every stage of the exercise.

1. Imagine entering a movie theatre. The screen is small and is located a long way away.
2. You take a seat right at the back of the theatre.
3. On the distant screen you can see an image of yourself before the incident and an image of yourself after the incident when you have recovered.
4. Both images are in black and white.

The Champion

5. Now imagine floating up out of your body and going into the projection room at the movie theatre. From here it will be possible to watch yourself watching a movie.

6. In the projection room you have complete control over everything, and shortly you will play a movie of the events that had traumatized you, viewing it from the first image of yourself to the second image of yourself.

7. Focus on the person sitting in front of you (yourself), so that you are watching someone watching a movie. This creates an additional step of distancing you from the events. While looking at the person in front of you, play the entire movie from the first image of yourself to the second image of yourself.

8. Once you have reached the end of the movie, go back down into your own body and then go all the way down to the screen and jump into the movie at the end.

9. Over 1.5 seconds, rewind at high speed the entire movie with you participating in the events. Trauma is an experience that moves forward, you were traumatized <u>after</u> the event. By rehearsing the incident

backwards you are practising experiencing the incident in a way which <u>undoes</u> the trauma.

10. Let your mind go blank, think of something completely different. What you ate today, what you want to do on the weekend, when will you meet with friends etc. Think of any random thing which is unrelated to what you are currently doing.

11. After a brief pause, repeat the exercise. About seven times should be sufficient to noticeably reduce the sense of anxiety you experience when thinking about the incident.

To do this process the first time usually takes quite a lot of time and concentration. As you become familiar with the process and as the trauma recedes, you will find it becomes easier and faster. After you have done the process a couple of times you can add background music to make the event seem even less important – try adding the theme song from some absurd comedy such as Monty-Python's Flying Circus, or imagine music from a 1920s silent movie.

If you are in a hurry and need to speed this process up, simply do the steps for rewinding the experience. MRI scans indicate that this step is sufficient to alter the neurology and can by itself reduce trauma.

To unlearn a habit

1. Imagine a small screen in front of you, about the size of a cell-phone screen 20-30 metres away from you.
2. See yourself performing the entire bad habit from start to finish in black and white.
3. Go into the experience and over 1.5 seconds experience doing the bad habit backwards.
4. Let your mind go blank and think about something completely different.
5. Repeat this exercise at least seven times.

To install a habit

1. Imagine seeing yourself performing the technique you want to develop.
2. See this as a large movie, close to you.
3. Make the images in the movie bright, clear and attractive
4. Having watched yourself performing the technique perfectly, step into the movie and play it again, with you participating in it. Imagine all of the sounds, the smells, the

feelings that you would be experiencing when you perform this technique in real life.

5. Having completed the movie, let your mind go blank.
6. Repeat this exercise at least seven times.

Time distortion:

1. See yourself in the third person (dissociated) performing your sport.
2. Make this movie as real as possible in terms of setting, size, and colours. Make the image large and close to you.
3. Notice how quickly you move and respond in comparison to your opponent.
4. After watching your performance for a while, let the image of you approach you and step into your body.
5. As he steps into your body, he brings with him all of the knowledge and skills he has and possesses, including the fast reactions, reflexes and ability to perform at a high level, really quickly.
6. Let this knowledge spread throughout your body, through every muscle, carried

through your blood to every cell and molecule.

7. Now visualise performing your sport again, but this time you are doing it from a first person point of view (associated). Your actions appear, look and feel to you to be occurring at a normal speed, but the actions of your opponents seem to be extremely slow, giving you time to respond to the situation easily.

8. Having spent some time enjoying this visualisation, let your mind go blank. Think about something else for a while. Repeat the entire process several times.

Belief changes

1. Think of the belief you want to remove, for example "I always crack under pressure".

2. Now think of the opposite, positive belief that you would like to have instead of the old negative belief. If your belief was "I always crack under pressure", this might be changed to "I stay focused and perform best when under pressure".

3. As you think about the negative belief let an image that represents that belief come to mind. Often this image will be an occasion

that justifies the belief, such as when you <u>did</u> crack under pressure.

4. As you see that image of the belief let it start to fade, become less distinct. Let the image start to shrink and move slowly away from you.

5. Let that image disappear into the distance and as it disappears let it be engulfed by a ball of flame so it is destroyed completely.

6. As the negative belief disappears over the horizon, let the image of the positive belief, starting out small, come flying towards you, as it gets closer it becomes bigger and bigger, more colourful and more real.

7. Bring the positive belief close to you so it sits in a space similar to what the old negative belief had.

8. Let your mind go blank. Think of something completely different for a few seconds then repeat the exercise so that you do it a total of seven times.

Masking

1. Write down the main characteristics or traits you want to have while performing your sport. (If you are in a high profile sport, you might also want to create a

The Champion

media mask for dealing with press conferences or journalists). For sport these might include patience, calmness, control, masterfulness, finesse, energy, aggression, confidence, ferocity, slyness, cunning, ... depending on your sport and what your normal personality seems to lack.

2. Imagine standing on the side-lines, preparing to go onto the field (enter the ring etc.) and imagine that you hold in your hands your sporting mask.

3. As you hold the mask in your hands you see each of the skills and personality traits you want to have when you are competing falling into your mask. Some people see this as words, others see these traits as actual representations of the trait in use – so if it is patience they see themselves being patient in a sporting setting, if it is aggression, they see themselves being aggressive.

4. Once all the personality traits have entered the mask, imagine placing it on your face, and even carry out the action, placing the imaginary mask on your face.

5. As the mask fits onto your face, visualise all the personality traits being carried through

your body, through every muscle and cell in your entire body.

6. Now view yourself performing in both a third person and first person (point of view), performing with this new performance personality.

Parts integration

1. Place your hands in front of you and ask the part generating the self-sabotaging behaviour to come out of you and sit/stand in your left hand. Ask yourself what does it look like? How does it feel? What temperature is it? Does it move? What size is it? People give a variety of answers, sometimes the part is large and heavy, sometimes small, sometimes it looks like them, often it looks like an unhappy version of themselves. In general there is a wide variety, so work with whatever options come to mind. Often people don't actually "see" or "feel" the part but answers just come to mind. Work with these. Once the part has come out, thank it for appearing and being prepared to "talk" with you.

2. Ask the part of you which wants to achieve your sporting goal and ask it to come out of

The Champion

you and sit/stand in your right hand. Ask yourself the same questions what does it look like? How does it feel? What temperature is it? Does it move? What size is it? The image which often appears for athletes is of them wearing a medal, or on a podium. Sometimes it is a cup representing victory. Representations vary from individual to individual. Once the part has come out, thank it for appearing and being prepared to "talk" with you.

3. Still focusing on that part in your right hand, tell it that you understand that it wants to help you. Ask it what its intention is. What does it want? Wait until some answer appears in your mind. Often it will appear to be extremely simple and prosaic.

4. Once you have the answer, ask it to imagine that it has that intention completely and fully, and having that intention completely and fully, ask it what it wants which is even more important. Wait until an answer comes to mind.

5. Continue asking this question. As you receive answers and reiterate the question you will find yourself going through a list of wants and desires that represent the

sort of person you are. Often when people finally reach the end of the iteration, they find that what they really want is happiness, peace, love, or a sense of oneness or wholeness. Once you have reached the final iteration ...

6. Turn your attention back to the part in your left hand, and tell it that you understand that it wants to help you. Ask it what it is trying to achieve through the behaviour (which you perceive as self-sabotage), ask it what its intention is. Wait until some answer appears in your mind. Often it will appear to be simple and prosaic.

7. Once you have the answer, ask it to imagine that it has that intention completely and fully, and having that intention completely and fully, ask it what it wants which is even more important. Wait until an answer comes to mind.

8. Continue asking this question until you start getting the same answers as you received for your right hand. This demonstrates to both parts that they have the same goals and aims and are simply working against each other to try to achieve them. Ask the part in the left hand

The Champion

if it recognizes this? Usually, it will. Sometimes it won't, in which case you need to continue following the intentions further until you reach the identical highest intention (peace, calm, etc).

9. When the two parts have agreed that they share the same intentions ask them if they can now work together to achieve the same goals. Often, at this point the left hand will be reluctant because it has very good reasons (as it perceives them) for generating self-sabotaging behaviour. You can then ask it what it needs in order to cooperate with your right hand. This is where you need to start negotiations and often your right hand will need to agree to some of the needs of the left hand.

10. Conduct the negotiations between the hand asking each what it wants and what it needs. They usually come to an agreement quite quickly.

11. Having agreed the two parts can then recognize that they can work together to achieve your sporting goals and you can then place your hands together. When they do come together people often see the parts merging and becoming a single representation. You can then let this

united, single part, return to your body. Some people visualize this process, others "place" it inside themselves by bringing their hands to their stomach, or to their heart.

Changing the voice in your head

1. Listen to the voice. Pay attention to what it is saying, notice the tone, the volume and the rhythm. Identify who is the voice in your head. Often these voices come from adults in our youth and are phrases, which we were frequently told. They can often also be voices which we heard when we were impressionable (for example going through difficult times in our lives, or under significant stress), coaches' and drill sergeants' voices often get imprinted as a result of this stress.

2. After identifying whose voice is talking to you, see them, observe their face and body language as they speak to you.

3. Expand the scope of what you can see to the context behind the events. Understand the reasons why they are talking to you the way they are. What does this reveal about them? How does it change the meaning of what they were telling you?

The Champion

4. Now imagine that you are talking to that person today and ask them what they really meant to say and what they wanted to do? What was their real intention? Thank them for trying to help.

5. Identify a trusted friend who cares for you and who encourages you the way you want to be encouraged. If you are unable to think of someone whose voice you would like to use, you can use either your own, or decide what sort of voice you would like to hear to encourage you.

6. Change voices. Ask the original person's voice, whether it would be prepared to use this other voice, which you will listen to attentively, it can always return to the old voice if the new one doesn't work.

Hypnotic induction

Lie back and relax and think of a time when you were really truly relaxed ... a time when you were on the point of sleep ... you know that feeling at the end of a long, tiring day when you lie down, tired, and think that you might just do something for a little while before going to sleep ... but your eyes close and almost instantly you fall away into a deep, deep sleep ... and just imagine doing that now, when I say relax ... and when I say relax, that means that you can relax totally ... fully taking the time to enjoy how the muscles in your neck and body start to lengthen... that's right, you can begin to feel that relaxation and as you notice how your muscles in your neck and shoulders relax you might notice that warmth spreading throughout your body ... and you might be wondering, after all its good to wonder ... and you might wonder just how relaxed you can become, now .... that's right, and take a deep breath in and turn your attention inwards ... as you really begin to enjoy the depth of your relaxation you can focus on the sound of my voice and that means you are falling deeper .... into another state, a deeper state where your mind can make changes ... and you don't mind, do you? After all, it is your mind ... And you may not even have noticed yet, how your breathing is slowing down ... just as you are slowing down inside ... That's right, and that means that you are going even deeper into trance, now. And as you go deeper into a state of trance, your conscious mind might like to wonder ... wonder what it was that I was saying four sentences ago ... and as you realise with amusement how hard it is to remember ... what it was that I said four or five sentences ago ... you might be surprised at how deeply you are in trance already ...

The Champion

That's right ... and as you wonder you may notice how slowly you are breathing ... which means that you are going even deeper into trance ... that's right ... and as you notice just how slowly you are breathing ... you might also notice that the sounds are becoming slower ... and that means that you are already in a deep ... deep trance... and you can continue to take that trance deeper still ... to a place deep inside where you are completely still ... that's right ... now ... you can find yourself in a place where change happens automatically ... and you can really focus on the sound of my voice...

And now ... when you think about your sport ...

Hypnotic Suggestions

Motivation: From now on, you will find that each day you train, the more fun you will have, and the more you train and participate in your sport, the easier you find it and the better you become, so that whenever you think about your sport and training for your sport, you are overcome with a strong desire to train, to become better and more focused.

Strength: Each time you train and compete, you will find that your muscles are stronger and more powerful. You have more force, more energy, more strength. You notice that performing tasks that were difficult becomes easier, and simpler. You notice that you have greater control, greater focus and accuracy... That's right, and your muscles are becoming both stronger and more flexible. And you will notice too, that your recovery time after training becomes significantly faster, while your body builds just the right sort of muscle that is needed for you to compete successfully in your sport and train successfully in your sport. As your muscles become stronger and more powerful, your body is becoming healthier and stronger too, any old injuries you had heal better and faster, old weaknesses can now become strengths and your body is becoming better,

The Champion

	healthier, more powerful and stronger...
Fear and anxiety:	As you consider that fear, that you have previously experienced, you can let your body relax and separate fear from reality, because you know that fear is just an emotion and emotional states can be changed... just as fear can change... when you were little, you were probably once afraid of the dark... but now, look at you... you are no longer afraid... and people sometimes want to hold onto fear, because they think that fear helps them, but if you think about it, about that fear that you had, how did it help you? Did it make you calm? Did it enable you to accurately assess the danger and to avoid it? Because, usually, people find that they deal with danger much better when they can assess danger rationally, and that they are safer and happier when they are calm... and this means that you can now release this fear, fully and completely,

release this negative emotion, let it wash away from you, filling you with calm and enabling you to rationally analyse any situation, that's right, looking after and protecting you by releasing that fear that you once had. That's right and so you can now let that fear go, let it fall into your past, forget that fear that you once had... forget it fully and completely.... So that you are no clear headed, focused, calm....that's right...

Going into flow

And whenever you compete in your sport, you can now perform at your very best. Whenever competing your body can relax and your subconscious takes over. Trained reactions and responses automatically take over and you effortlessly perform at your best. And when we say, "your best" we really mean better than you ever imagined, moving fluidly, softly, powerfully, letting your intuition and subconscious mind guide you to performing

The Champion

better and better... and the more you practice, the better you become... easily going into the zone, into the flow of perfect performance...

Positivity And from time to time you may have had doubts about yourself, about what you can do and whether it is worth continuing... whether you are in the gym, or jogging or in the middle of a competition... or relaxing after dinner in the comfort of your house... you might sometimes have doubts... whenever such a doubt comes to you, you can feel a new burst of energy, a new sense of determination and instead of asking questions like "is it worth it?", "can I go on?", in the back of the mind you can hear a voice urging you on "Come on, let's do this! You can do this!"... That's right... and when of the great things about doing sport is the sense of positivity and confidence that builds within you whenever you train and compete... and you can let this positivity flow on and beyond your sport, so it touches other elements of your life, seeping into and overwhelming other areas of your life, making you more positive, more motivated, more inspired and inspiring in your sport and in life, in general...

Time distortion And you know that time is relative.... And so is our perception of time.... Sometimes when you are bored, time seems to slow.... And sometimes when we are with friends, having a good time... it seems to fly... And you will have noticed too, after driving a car along the highway or motorway and you need to slow down... it all seems incredibly slow... and that means that you become accustomed to slowing fast things down... and you can do that now... when doing your sport, slow down the external world, so that you can respond even faster to what's happening.... That's right.... And what's more,

The Champion

when you are having fun, it makes sense to slow things down, so you can enjoy more of what you love... that's right....

Injury recovery

And now as you consider that injury that you received, you can leave the emotions and the disappointment behind you... forget about the unpleasantness... that's right... and let your body and subconscious now focus on how quickly you can heal and recover. That's right... because your body knows how to recover quickly and easily... pumping additional blood to injured muscles... sending nutrients, healing old injuries, letting the muscles relax and recover quickly... and as you start to think about how quickly former injuries can heal, recover and strengthen, you might even notice a tingling pulsing in the muscle as the recovery begins to accelerate now... and you might feel a warmth in your muscles, tendons and ligaments as they heal and become healthier, stronger, now recovering.... And as you think now about the injury that you received, you can now throw it out along with other unneeded junk, let any old trauma, recollections of the injury fade from your memory and disappears... and the more you let go of that old injury now, the easier and faster your body can recover, bringing more nutrients and blood to heal and increase recovery, so that the muscle tingles and feels warm with the rapid recovery... and you can remember how good you feel when your muscles, tendons and ligaments are in top physical condition, strong and elastic.

Parts Integration for pain control

1. Place your hands in front of you and ask the part, generating the pain to come out of you and sit/stand in your left hand. Ask yourself what does it look like? How does it feel? What temperature is it? Does it

The Champion

move? What size is it? People give a variety of answers, sometimes the part is large and heavy, sometimes small, sometimes it looks like them, often it looks like an unhappy version of them. In general there is a wide variety, work with whatever options come to mind. Often people don't actually "see" or "feel" the part but answers just come to mind. Work with these. Once the part has come out, thank it for appearing and being prepared to "talk" with you.

2. Ask the part of you which wants to continue what you are doing and ask it to come out of you and sit/stand in your right hand. Ask yourself what does it look like? How does it feel? What temperature is it? Does it move? What size is it? Once the part has come out, thank it for appearing and being prepared to "talk" with you.

3. Still focusing on that part in your right hand, tell it that you understand that it wants to help you. Ask it what its intention is? What does it want? Wait until some answer appears in your mind. Often it will appear to be extremely simple and prosaic.

4. Once you have the answer, ask it to imagine that it has that has that intention

completely and fully, and having that intention completely and fully, ask it what it wants which is even more important. Wait until an answer comes to mind.

5. Continue asking this question. As you receive answers and reiterate the question you will find yourself going through a list of wants and desires that represent the sort of person you are. Often when people finally reach the end of the iteration, they find that what they really want is happiness, peace, love, or a sense of oneness or wholeness. Once you have reached the final iteration ...

6. Turn your attention to the part, which is in your left hand, and tell it that you understand that it wants to help you. Ask it what it is trying to achieve through the pain (which you perceive as self-sabotage), ask it what its intention is. Wait until some answer appears in your mind. Often it will appear to be extremely simple and prosaic.

7. Once you have the answer, ask it to imagine that it has that intention completely and fully, and ask it what it wants which is even more important. Wait until an answer comes to mind.

The Champion

8. Continue asking this question until you start getting the same answers as you received for your right hand. This demonstrates to both parts that they have the same goals and aims and are simply working against each other to try to achieve them. Ask the part in the left hand if it recognizes this? Usually, it will. Sometimes it won't, in which case you need to continue following the intentions further until you reach the identical highest intention (peace, calm, etc).

9. When the two parts have agreed that they share the same intentions ask them if they can now work together to achieve the same goals. Often, at this point the left hand will be reluctant because it has very good reasons (as it perceives them) for making you feel the pain. You can then ask it what it needs in order to cooperate with your right hand. This is where you need to start negotiations and often your right hand will need to agree to some of the needs of the left hand.

10. Conduct the negotiations between the hand asking each what it wants and what it needs. They usually come to an agreement quite quickly.

11. Having agreed the two parts can then recognize that they can work together you can then place your hands together. When they do come together people often see the parts merging and becoming a single representation. You can then let this united, single part, return to your body.

Altering representation of pain

1. Ask yourself a series of questions:
    a. Where is the pain?
    b. What shape is the pain?
    c. What colour is the pain?
    d. Is the pain moving? If so how is it moving? Is it pulsating, spinning, throbbing?
    e. Is it a sharp pain or dull pain?
    f. Is it hot or cold?
2. Change the severity of the pain. Initially try making the pain hurt more to demonstrate to yourself that it is possible to use your imagination to change the degree of pain you experience. Now, imagine the pain as being less painful.

The Champion

3. Start altering some of these pain properties. This is a process of experimentation, some changes will reduce the pain, others will intensify the pain. Experiment and find which representations give you greatest pain relief.

4. Often people depict pain as being a jagged object, sharp and pointed. Experiment, and see if you can alter the shape of the pain from something sharp and pointed to something soft and round. Notice how this alters your perception of the sensations.

5. Change the colour of the pain. Often people represent pain as being red, change it to a soothing green, or blue. Some people like to change the pain to gold or silver (colours often associated with love). Try using different colours and notice what difference it makes to your experience of the sensations.

6. Change how the pain is moving. If the pain is still, try moving it in a certain direction. If it is moving, make it move in the opposite direction, or make it sit still in one position. Notice how this alters the way you experience the sensations.

7. Change the temperature of the pain. Cool it down or increase the temperature and notice the difference it makes.

8. Change where the pain is located. You can now experiment moving the pain around your body. If you have abdominal pain, move it to another part of the abdomen. If you have knee pain, move it up into your thigh or down into your calf.

Alter subconscious perception:

1. Think of a skill that you would like to improve. A basketball player might like to make shooting for the net easier, a soccer or hockey player might want to make shooting for goal easier, a bowler at cricket might want to make it easier to bowl a batsman out, a runner might want to make long distances easier to run, etc.

2. Once you know what you want to make easier, think of what would make that skill easier. Usually this involves making the target or the goal bigger, so if you are a hockey player wanting to make it easier to score a goal, you imagine a large goal,

The Champion

which is impossible to miss. If you are a goalie, you might want to increase your own size and decrease the size of the goal so that it is easier to protect. Archers and target shooters can imagine the target being closer and larger. For fencing, I imagine competitors with large target areas and very short arms. A tennis player might like to increase the size of the opponent's court and decrease the size of the opponent and his/her own court, so it is perceived as being easier to defend.

3. Once you have an image you want to use, visualise competing and training with the new representations, seeing yourself striking the target (or achieving whatever skill you want to achieve) easily, over and over again.

4. After you have spent some time (maybe a minute or so) visualising point 3, let your mind go blank. Think about something completely different for maybe half a minute (think about going for a walk, what you want to do on the weekend, when you get home, etc.) Then repeat the visualisation. Do this seven times. The more you do it, the more effective this

should be, but seven times is sufficient to get some benefit from the exercise.

5. Go out and test how well this has worked.

Bibliography and further reading

Andreas, Steve and Connirae, *Heart of the Mind, Engaging Your Inner Power to Change With NLP Neuro-Linguistic Programming,* Real People Press 1989

Boulter, Simon, *The Gymless Body: Become the Gym*, 2012

Bush, Anthony, *Foundations in Sports Science,* Heinemann Educational Books, 2012

Christensen, Loren W., *Mental Rehearsal for Warriors: For Cops, Soldiers and Martial Artists*, 2014

Christensen, Loren W., *Speed Training: How To Develop Your Maximum Speed For Martial Arts*, Paladin Press, 1996

Divine, Mark, *Unbeatable Mind: Forge Resiliency and Mental Toughness to Succeed at an Elite Level,* 2014

Dotz, T., Hoobyar, T., Sanders, S., *NLP: The Essential Guide to Neuro-Linguistic Programming,* William Morrow Paperbacks, 2013.

Ferriss, Timothy, *The 4-Hour Body: An uncommon guide to rapid fat-loss, incredible sex and becoming superhuman,* Ebury Digital, 2011

Garratt, Ted, *Sporting Excellence: Optimising Sports Performance Using NLP,* Crown House Publishing, 2001

Gray, Dr. Richard M., "NLP and PTSD: the Visual-Kinesthetic Dissociation Protocol", *Current Research in NLP: vol 2 - Proceedings of 2010 Conference.* At time of writing the article could be found at: http://www.anlp.org/files/nlp-and-ptsd-the-visual-kinesthetic-dissociation-protocol_6_331.pdf;

Grossman, Lt. Col. Dave, *On Killing,* Open Road Media; Revised edition, 2014.

The Champion

Kalym, Ashley, *Complete Calisthenics: The Ultimate Guide To Bodyweight Exercise*, Ashley Kalym, 2014

MacKenzie, Brian, *Power Speed ENDURANCE: A Skill-Based Approach to Endurance Training*, Victory Belt Publishing, 2012

McDougall, Christopher, *Born to Run: The hidden tribe, the ultra-runners, and the greatest race the world has never seen*, Profile Books, 2010

McDougall, Christopher, *Natural Born Heroes: How a Daring Band of Misfits Mastered the Lost Secrets of Strength and Endurance*, Knopf, 2015

McNab, Andy, *Immediate Action*, Transworld Digital, 2008

O'Connor, Joseph, *NLP and Sport*, Thorsons, 2001

Powers, John, *Calisthenics: The 20-Minute Dream Body with Bodyweight Exercises and Calisthenics*, Calisthenics for beginners, 2015

Richardson, Alan, "Mental Practice: A Review and Discussion", *Research Quarterly*, American Association for Health, Physical Education and Recreation Volume 38, Issue 1, 1967.

Rushall, Brent S., and Pyke, Frank S, *Training for Sports and Fitness*, MacMillan Publishers Australia, 1990

Scott, Jason, *Bodyweight Training: Rapid Muscluar Enhancement Using Bodyweight Only Training*, 2014

Tsatsouline, Pavel, *Power to the People!: Russian Strength Training Secrets for Every American,* Dragon Door Publications, 2014

Tsatsouline, Pavel, *The Naked Warrior: Master the Secrets of the super-Strong--Using Bodyweight Exercises Only,* Dragon Door Publications, 2003

Tucker, Cole, *Killer Athletes: America's Special Operations Warriors Share Lessons & Advice To Help Young Athletes Become Champions!*, CreateSpace Independent Publishing Platform, 2014

Other works by Peter D Campbell
In My Brother's Shadow – drama

An absorbing and skilful story, exploring the attitudes of a younger brother who has grown up overawed by the image of his elder brother who went missing in Yugoslavia ten years earlier. In his attempt to break away from a monotonous mild-class lifestyle the main hero goes on pilgrimage to Bosnia and Serbia to explore the land that took his brother's life. The story takes him to the cold and imperial beauty of St. Petersburg, Russia, where events force him to re-examine the basis of his morality, the nature of war and peace, love and hate, and violence and submission. It explores the motivations behind these and how ordinary people can be pushed to do the unthinkable. *In my Brother's Shadow* explores the relationship of two brothers and how actions can be defined by their environment.

Purchase it from www.amazon.com/dp/B00MCY6RYU

Peter D. Campbell

Language Learning Secrets Revealed: How Anyone can Learn a Language
Discover the secrets the professionals use!

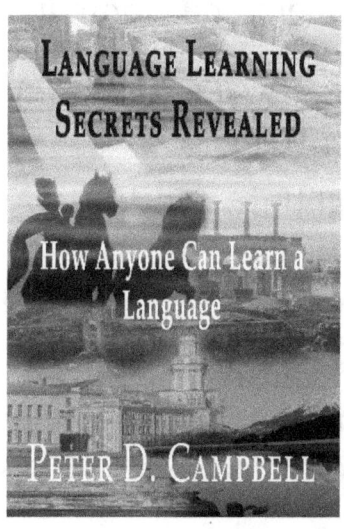

This is a practical book for all those who would like to learn a language. It includes techniques for learning, key information about the structure of language and how to learn it, motivational techniques, principles for accelerated learning, and skills used by memory athletes and linguists. Regardless of your language skills and past experience with learning foreign languages, I will show you the best techniques for learning languages and improving your current knowledge of a foreign language.

Whether you are a complete beginner or a competent speaker this book will reveal techniques that will enable you to master material better and enhance your skills.

This book will teach you to go from beginner to fluent in six months.

Purchase it from Amazon: www.amazon.com/dp/B00OBM3AXC

The Champion

Purrfect Tales – satire

This remarkable book explores what you have always known but never quite understood - how it is that your favourite puss went from being your cat to your master.

A delightful and witty account, "Purrfect Tales" retells key events in mythology, legend and history to reveal the subtle influence of the velvet paw in every area of human endeavour.

Purchase it from www.amazon.com/dp/B00MCY79GK

Peter D. Campbell

The Prostitute and the Beggar

Enigmatic private eye John Marlot looks into the sudden disappearance of a Picasso painting from one of the world's largest art galleries and dives into the depths Russia's criminal underworld.

Purchase it from Amazon: www.amazon.com/dp/B00MCY78CA

The Prodigal Son

Private eye John Marlot investigates the disappearance of an oil tycoon's son in St. Petersburg and soon finds himself looking at the darker side of romance in Russia's northern capital.

Purchase it from Amazon: www.amazon.com/dp/B00OHW3SQK

The Blizzard by Alexander Pushkin

In a delightful tale by Russia's greatest writer, mystery surrounds a lovely and delightful young woman who refuses despite everything to marry the man of her dreams. Peter D Campbell has retranslated Pushkin's timeless classic making a compelling and accessible text.

Purchase it from www.amazon.com/dp/B00MCY6VCI

The Shot by Alexander Pushkin

A chilling story of romance and vengeance by Russia's greatest writer, Alexander Pushkin. This modern translation by Peter D Campbell brings out the full mastery of Pushkin's tale which will grip readers young and old alike.

Purchase it from www.amazon.com/dp/B00MCY7HHQ

www.ingramcontent.com/pod-product-compliance
Lightning Source LLC
Chambersburg PA
CBHW071247230426
43668CB00011B/1629